D0467412

From Here to Enlightenment

From Here to Enlightenment

AN INTRODUCTION TO TSONG-KHA-PA'S CLASSIC TEXT
The Great Treatise on the Stages of the Path to Enlightenment

His Holiness the Dalai Lama

Translated, edited, and annotated by
Guy Newland

SNOW LION
BOSTON & LONDON
2012

Snow Lion
An imprint of Shambhala Publications, Inc.
Horticultural Hall
300 Massachusetts Avenue
Boston, Massachusetts 02115
www.shambhala.com

9 8 7 6 5 4 3 2 1

First Edition
Printed in the United States of America

♾ This edition is printed on acid-free paper that meets the American National Standards Institute z39.48 Standard.
♻ Shambhala makes every attempt to print on recycled paper.
For more information please visit www.shambhala.com.

Distributed in the United States by Random House, Inc., and in Canada by Random House of Canada Ltd

Designed by Gopa & Ted2, Inc.

Library of Congress Cataloging-in-Publication Data

Bstan-'dzin-rgya-mtsho, Dalai Lama XIV, 1935–
From here to enlightenment: an introduction to Tsong-kha-pa's
classic text The great treatise on the stages of the path to enlightenment /
His Holiness the Dalai Lama; translated, edited, and annotated
by Guy Newland.
p. cm.
Summary: "In 2008, to commemorate the completion of the English translation of Tsong-kha-pa's classic text 'Great Treatise on the Stages of the Path to Enlightenment' (Tib. Lam Rim Chen Mo), the Dalai Lama gave a six-day teaching on this text at Lehigh University. 'From Here to Enlightenment' makes this momentous event available for a wider general readership. The basic topics of Buddhism are woven together for his Western audience. With dependent relatedness as the primary theme of the teachings, the Dalai Lama explores this from various viewpoints throughout the book. True to the Dalai Lama's profound sense of compassion, these fundamental issues of Buddhism are always presented within the context of basic human values and concerns"— Provided by publisher.
ISBN: 978-1-55939-382-9 (hardcover)
1. Tsoṅ-kha-pa Blo-bzaṅ-grags-pa, 1357–1419. Lam rim chen mo.
2. Lam-rim. I. Newland, Guy. II. Title.
BQ7645.L35B7628 2012
294.3'442—dc23
2011029803

Contents

Editor's Preface

THE DALAI LAMA here invites you to join him in studying one of the very greatest works of his tradition: Tsong-kha-pa's *Great Treatise on the Stages of the Path to Enlightenment.* When he fled Tibet on a cold March night in 1959, he couldn't carry much—but he was careful to take this book. Synthesizing the vast corpus of earlier Buddhist teachings on the path, Tsong-kha-pa's monumental work functions by design both as incisive philosophy and personal spiritual counsel. This is the first time the Dalai Lama has taught this text in the West. Given at Lehigh University in July of 2008, His Holiness's teachings were occasioned by the publication in three volumes of the first complete English translation of the *Great Treatise* (Ithaca, N.Y.: Snow Lion Publications, 2001, 2002, and 2004).

Published in 1402, Tsong-kha-pa's *Great Treatise* is a landmark work that defines and defends against alternatives a highly distinctive interpretation of emptiness as the ultimate reality. In the history of Tibetan Buddhism it has been both highly controversial and highly influential. But in teaching it here, the Dalai Lama does not focus on sectarian controversies. Instead of presenting Tsong-kha-pa's views as refutations of inferior alternatives, he demonstrates how they are integral to the vast Tibetan wisdom tradition. Crediting the heritage of this tradition entirely to the sages of India, he links its insights to our universal human situation.

The Dalai Lama guides us through the *Great Treatise* with grace, humor, passion, and utter mastery, weaving his explanations around a single, profound theme: *dependent arising*, the notion that all things arise and exist *only* through deep interconnections. Chapter after chapter, he returns to this theme, exploring every aspect of the path in the light of this teaching. To give some examples: at the outset His Holiness teaches global responsibility, emphasizes that in the contemporary world it is especially clear that our destinies on this planet are bound together—no one person or nation can find happiness while neglecting others. Stressing the value of all world religions for the great majority of their traditional followers, he nonetheless points out that the distinctively Buddhist understanding of interdependence precludes belief in an uncaused Divine Creator. This is because *everything* exists only through its connections to and dependence upon other things. At the same time, he stresses the need to develop a strong conviction that our choices matter, our actions have moral consequences, through the dependent arising of karmic cause and effect. He places under analytical scrutiny the interdependent processes through which our grasping at a distorted sense of self leads us through cycles of needless misery. Again and again, he shows us how basic Buddhist ideas such as the three jewels and the four noble truths become deeply meaningful when comprehended from within a deep understanding of how all things are empty of any existence apart from dependent arising. He explores how love, compassion, and kindness depend upon a vivid experience of our deep connections and interdependent relationships with one another. Finally, offering a comparison to quantum physics, he introduces us to the profound idea that reality itself can never be *objectively* established, but exists only in the interrelatedness of an experiencing mind and its objects.

This book itself is another instance of dependent arising. It arises from teachings that depend on numberless causes and conditions, including the life work of Geshe Ngawang Wangyal, the many dedicated friends of the Tibetan Buddhist Learning Center, and the efforts of faculty, staff, students, and administrators at Lehigh University. I am most grateful to those who helped make this volume what it is, especially Geshe Thupten Jinpa, whose brilliant oral translation into English was absolutely crucial in formulating this work, and the Venerable Geshe Lhaktor and his assistant Tsering Gyatso, who transcribed the Tibetan of His Holiness's teachings. Joshua Cutler, Diana Cutler, the Venerable Geshe Yeshe Thapkay, the Venerable Thubten Chodron, Steven Rhodes, Gareth Sparham, Natalie Hauptman, Thomas Griffin, and Susan Higginbotham each gave crucial support, in various ways, when I needed it.

Since His Holiness's teachings are an explanation of the *Great Treatise* for English speakers, I cite his frequent references to it within the main body of the text by placing in parentheses the volume number and page number of the Snow Lion Publications English translation. I have annotated His Holiness's teachings with explanatory notes and bibliographic references primarily to English translations of the many other texts that he cites. Because this work is intended for the general reader, I have chosen not to use standard diacritical markings in rendering Sanskrit words and I have preferred to render Tibetan names and terms in an approximate phonetic form rather than with transliteration.

Foreword

I AM HONORED to welcome this amazing book. In it, His Holiness the Great Fourteenth Dalai Lama of Tibet (b. 1935) gives a concise but comprehensive teaching of the quintessential instructions that are set forth in magnificent detail by Jey Rinpoche, Tsong Khapa Losang Drakpa (1357-1419) in his *Great Treatise on the Stages of the Path to Enlightenment.* Tsong Khapa wrote the work in 1402, in the fourth year after his complete enlightenment, high in the Yama-tongue Cave on the Oeudey Gungyal Mountain above the hermitage at Olkha, where he had spent his five-year retreat. During the subsequent years he was bent on only one thing—to fashion the liberative teachings of the Buddha and his numerous successors up to Atisha (982-1054) into a high-efficiency escalator of a path to enlightenment, accessible to the widest possible variety of human beings. In the beginning of the current century this great work was marvelously translated into English by the students of the Venerable Geshe Wangyal. To celebrate that work, in 2008 His Holiness came to the United States and gave an introduction to the practices, which is beautifully recorded in this *From Here to Enlightenment.* I was fortunate to be present at Lehigh University when that happened; but reading this book now, I am astounded at how much I missed at the time—it is like looking into a multifaceted clear jewel with a stronger magnifying glass: when the teaching is before you in a text you can see more shapely depths and more beautiful reflections.

It gives you everything you need to enter upon the great stages of the path. Yet it is short and simple, never over the head of a beginner, while at the same time challenging the more experienced student into renewed inquiry and deeper insight and refinement. It is the kind of concise quintessence that could only be delivered by this truly great teacher of the potentials and realities of human wisdom and compassion.

At the beginning of the *Great Stages*, Tsong Khapa himself goes into the details of the greatness of the teaching it transmits, which he received from his illustrious predecessor, Atisha, through the seminal works *Lamp of the Enlightenment Path* and *Stages of the Enlightenment Path*, which were fundamental to the Kadam order of Tibetan Buddhism. One of the warrants of the greatness of a teaching is the greatness of the teacher, and Atisha's greatness is clear from his biography, his huge impact on India and Tibet, and especially from the legacy he left in the form of the "Four-Square Path" to an authentic reception of the Buddha's teachings. The corners of this square are: 1) all teachings are to be understood as free of contradictions; 2) all discourses take effect as practical instructions; 3) the Victor's intention is thus easy to discover; and 4) thereby the abyss of abandoning the Dharma is avoided. A thousand years later this four-square path remains the surefire way to avoid sectarianism in Buddhism, and His Holiness the Dalai Lama is the living exemplar of staying fair and squarely on it, as he amply demonstrates in this precious work. His Holiness' own practice, unclaimed but evident attainment, and careful, eloquent communication come clearly through this work and open wide the door for the student to embark on the Stages of the Great Path!

His Holiness begins by sharing his own three main life commitments: as a human being, upholding the essential human values of intelligence and compassion; as a Buddhist monk, who wholeheartedly embraces within the principles of the four-square path all the great religious traditions outside Buddhism, mentioning especially Judaism, Christianity, and Islam, and even the spiritual traditions of secular humanism; and as a Tibetan, who seeks peaceful reconciliation with all people, reaching out with love and understanding especially to the Chinese people, who on an ordinary human level would count as Tibet's worst enemies.

Further, within Buddhism, he explains how he respects as elder the Theravada teachings, which he calls the Pali tradition, and the Mahayana traditions, which he calls the Sanskrit tradition, within which he counts the Chinese Buddhists also as his elders. But then he proclaims both Tsong Khapa and himself to be heirs of the Indian Buddhist Nalanda University tradition, descending from Nāgārjuna, Ārya Asanga, and others, and shares with us the intense joy he derives from opportunities of teaching Indian students and returning their long lost intellectual and spiritual treasures to their minds and hearts:

> I am especially moved, so very deeply touched, when I have the chance to give Buddhist teachings to Indian Buddhists. Everywhere in the world that I go to teach, my whole message is nothing but ancient Indian thought. That's all there is. For example, the message of nonviolence, ahimsa—this is the Indian tradition. And everything I am teaching here about the path to enlightenment—this is the treasure of the Nalanda tradition. When I teach my Indian friends, I think of how we kept alive in Tibet the treasure that they largely lost over the centuries. It gives me an incredible feeling of happiness to return this to them. (p. 20)

Reading this passage forcefully reminded me about how urgently His Holiness (along with the late Geshe Wangyal) wants us all to see to the translation of the library of Nalanda University, the works of its great Pandita scholar/practitioners that are collected in the Tibetan Tengyur, into English, Chinese, and modern Indic and European languages. Finally, he acknowledges how Tsong Khapa's *Great Stages* illuminates Atisha's organization of the path, building on how it had already been beautifully deployed by the Kagyu master Gampopa (1079-1153), the Sakya master Sapan (1182-1251), and the Nyingma master Longchenpa (1308-1364), thus showing the harmony between Tsong Khapa's *Great Stages* and the core teachings of the other main Tibetan Buddhist traditions.

Turning to the actual teachings of the path, His Holiness goes through the whole set of themes that Atisha and Tsong Khapa have drawn forth from the Sutras as central to the individual's development: the preciousness of human life and its purpose, coarse and subtle impermanence and immediacy of death, the workings of karmic causality, the inevitability of suffering in the egoistic life-cycle, the magnificence and blissfulness of universal compassion as it opens up into the spirit of enlightenment of the bodhisattva, and the all-important highest teaching of the transcendent wisdom of selflessness, emptiness, and universal relativity (dependent origination or arising, and dependent designation). In all of this, chapter by chapter, he extracts the quintessence of each stage and shares it so generously in such a concise way; it is positively breathtaking in its precision and sweep. Periodically, just as he did when he personally delivered the teaching, he pauses and responds to big questions from typical students and practitioners, which very much adds to the accessibility of the ideas taught.

In the last few chapters, His Holiness works smoothly through the complexities of some of the main Centrist (Mādhyamika) philosophers, such as Nāgārjuna, Āryadeva, Chandrakīrti, Shāntarakshita, and Tsong Khapa, and the subtleties of the dialectical (Prāsangika) and dogmatic (Svātantrika) interpretations of emptiness and the two realities, conventional and ultimate. He actually makes these topics clear and understandable, at least giving enough orientation to motivate the student to inquire further more deeply. And he ends with a hearty encouragement and the invitation to us all to undertake the journey on the path to our own Buddhahood, not just holding that out as something other people have, or some other great masters have attained, but urging us to aim for the inconceivably free and joyful way of being that we all have access to by developing the potential clear light blissful wisdom latent in the mind of each of us, whether we are Buddhist or not.

In conclusion, if the greatness of a teaching is important to motivate us to study it, and the greatness of its teacher is an important clue to that greatness, then the greatness of this world teacher, the Buddhist monk Tenzin Gyatso, His Holiness the Great Fourteenth Dalai Lama, as exquisitely revealed in this concise and lucid book, is a really important clue to the still unfailing vitality of these stages of the path to full enlightenment, helpful to open-minded people of all faiths or nonfaiths in the pluralistic spiritual culture of our world era.

Robert A. F. Thurman
Jey Tsong Khapa Professor of Indo-Tibetan
Buddhist Studies, Columbia University
President, Tibet House US

Ganden Dekyi Ling
Woodstock, New York
May 31, 2012
Saga Dawa, Tibetan Royal Water Dragon Year 2139

CHAPTER ONE

Deep Connections

GOOD AFTERNOON, everybody. Indeed I am very, very happy to be here to lecture on the *Great Treatise on the Stages of the Path to Enlightenment* (*lam rim chen mo*).[1] I visited the late Geshe Wangyal's center during my first visit to America in 1979 because, especially since the time of the Third Dalai Lama, there have long been very close links between Tibetans and Mongolians.[2] Tibetans have a unique and very close relationship with Mongolians, including the Kalmyks and Buryats. In my own case, one of my best study partners was Ngodrup Tsokyi, a Mongolian. He helped me so much, so I feel a very close, personal connection. One time when I visited the late Geshe Wangyal's center, we reflected on the many stories of our strong connections in the past. Everyone was deeply moved and we were all in tears together.

Joshua Cutler, Director of the Tibetan Buddhist Learning Center, is neither Tibetan nor Mongolian; he is European American. But I do think Joshua and Diana have very faithfully carried on the late Geshe Wangyal's spirit. They asked me to teach the *Great Treatise on the Stages of the Path to Enlightenment* and they translated it into English. I promised that in the future I would teach this text. Today, that is realized.

But of course this book is quite thick. Reading it all in a few days is impossible. So I will teach primarily by summarizing its essential points, elaborating as necessary.

The *Great Treatise* was written by Lama Tsong-kha-pa, a great scholar, a real holder of the Nalanda tradition.[3] I think he is one of the very best Tibetan scholars. Although it is now widely available in

Tibetan as well as English, you see that I brought with me today my own personal copy of this text. On March 17th, 1959, when I left Norbulingka that night, I brought this book with me.[4] Since then, I have used it ten or fifteen times to give teachings, all from this copy. So this is something very dear to me.

Global Responsibility

Most of you are familiar with my commitments, my views and thoughts. But perhaps some of you are new, so I want to mention briefly my basic commitments. In the first place, I am just one human being among six billion. The fact is that all six billion human beings share one planet. We all survive under one sun. Today, especially, we are simply one community in the face of population growth, instantaneous communication, the modern global economy, and our common environmental problems. We are really one entity. In reality, there is no separate, independent, individual interest. For each of us, the future is entirely dependent on the rest of humanity, the rest of the world. But our ways of thinking about things are still based on concepts inherited from ancient times when each community lived more or less independently. There is a growing gap between our perceptions and reality. Our outdated way of thinking gives us the mistaken view that we—and our communities—are separate from the rest of the world. Based on that, our actions are unrealistic.

Nobody wants more problems. Nonetheless, there are many problems and many of them we create for ourselves because we lack a holistic, realistic view. In order to develop a sense of global responsibility, we have to look at the entire planet. It is just one small planet and our individual futures entirely depend upon it. We must take care of it. The only way to safeguard our futures as individuals is to develop a sense of concern for the well-being of all other people, all of the other living beings in the world.

So my primary commitment is to make it clear that we need a sense of global responsibility. In this regard, I consider Buddhist teachings not as a religion, but simply as some ideas that may be helpful. It is useful, for example, to consider *all* living beings. Maybe it seems unrealistic to think about other beings in other worlds. Whether you think it makes sense or not, emotionally it is *very* useful. When we have been practicing extending our concern to an infinite number of beings on an infinite number of planets, then of course there is no question that we would want to care for six billion human beings right here on this planet. And billions of animals—they really suffer immensely at human hands, don't they? So the Buddhist message of infinite altruism is very relevant. It is not about our future lifetimes or becoming enlightened. It is simply that infinite altruism is very useful for becoming a happier person, a sensible and useful person on this planet.[5]

In day-to-day life, whenever we are facing difficulty, some of these Buddhist ideas can be really helpful. They equip our minds, particularly our emotions, so that we can maintain peace of mind when we are facing difficulty. This is good for our health. Too many worries and too much ambition are bound to increase suspicion and jealousy, leading to even more mental disturbance. Some of these Buddhist ideas can be very helpful to the well-being of individuals, mentally and emotionally. And in dependence upon that, they have physical benefits as well. So if you are a nonbeliever who has no interest in religion, fine. Listen to some of these ideas and if you hear something that seems useful, then take it. If you it feel that is nonsense, then just forget it.

Religious Harmony

My second commitment is to promote religious harmony. I am a Buddhist; sometimes I am considered a staunch Buddhist. Those ancient Indian Buddhist masters, particularly the scholars of Nalanda University, had very, very critical minds.[6] They analyzed everything, both the Buddha's own words and the views of non-Buddhist traditions. Buddhist masters like Nagarjuna, Aryadeva, Dignaga, Dharmakirti, and Shantarakshita were very sharp logicians who were able to find every crack, every weakness, in non-Buddhist philosophical positions. I am like this, at least to some degree. I want to investigate, to analyze, and in that sense I can say that I am a very staunch Buddhist.

At the same time, I also accept the value or potential of all of the major traditions. It is so terrible, so sad, that there is conflict in the name of religion. Innocent, genuine, faithful people suffer as a result. So it is essential to make an effort to promote religious harmony within a sense of respect and mutual understanding. It helps for non-Buddhists to understand something about the structure of Buddhism and for Buddhists to understand other religions.

This is why, yesterday, I went on pilgrimage in Rajasthan to the Ajmer Sharif shrine, a famous Muslim holy place.[7] It is perhaps the holiest place of Sufi Islam. Each year, prayers are offered for six days to commemorate the death of a great saint. They invited me. They prayed all night, but I preferred to participate in the early morning. So yesterday from 2:30 to 4:30 A.M. I prayed while wearing a Muslim hat—a Buddhist monk's robe and a Muslim hat.[8] There seemed to be several hundred thousand people and it was incredibly hot and humid. Of course, with so many people packed in a small area, there was sweat and odor. Maybe we can call it the scent of ethical discipline—mixed, of course, with sweat! My robes are still damp right now. I really enjoyed this; it was wonderful.

A few weeks earlier there was an international Muslim conference in Delhi. They invited me and I think I was the only non-Muslim participating. That afternoon, I visited the Jamma Masjid in Delhi and prayed together with thousands and thousands of Muslims.[9] That was the first time I wore the Muslim white cap. Personally, this made me very happy, but I felt a little hesitant because I thought that perhaps some conservative elements might feel differently about my doing this. But the response from the mainstream community was excellent. It seems that people appreciated my efforts to promote inter-religious harmony and genuine respect across the traditions.

If you also think that this issue of understanding and harmony across the world religions is important, then please take action. Make closer contacts with the followers of other traditions. Since the September

11th event, it is extremely important to reach out to Muslim brothers and sisters, to make contact with them. Many people have a negative impression of Muslims and that is totally wrong.

Of course, in the past, many Indian Buddhists did suffer a great deal at the hands of Muslims, but the past is gone.[10] It is useless to dwell on this and to hold on to hatred. It is absolutely foolish. Today, for example, there are many Muslims living in the Bodhgaya area. I think that perhaps their ancestors came to Bodhgaya in order to destroy the Buddhist temple there.[11] But now they are the best friends of Buddhist pilgrims. Whenever I visit Bodhgaya they welcome me with tea and some very delicious nuts. I always enjoy that. That is the reality today. There are thousands of Muslims there; they are very genuine practitioners of Islam and wonderful human beings.

China and Tibet

My third commitment is to the cause of Tibet and its people and culture. Until there is a mutually beneficial understanding between Tibetans and Chinese, it's my moral responsibility to speak for Tibetans. Unfortunately, since the crisis of March 10, 2008, Chinese government propaganda has given many Chinese the sense that Tibetans are anti-Chinese.[12] Feelings were running high. During my last visit to America, some Chinese were demonstrating where I was speaking, so I wanted to meet some of them. I did meet seven of them. Two of them calmly listened to my explanations, but the rest were very angry and had no interest in listening. The emotions involved are just too strong.

I suggested that now is a perfect time to set up friendship groups joining Tibetans with Han Chinese wherever they live in the same communities. They should get to know each other so that when a problem arises, they can discuss it, exchanging information and perspective. Without this, there is usually no communication between these groups. They remain isolated and then, when there is an incident, emotions overwhelm them.

You can help. In any community where there are some Tibetans and some Han Chinese, help them to create a common friendship group. You can join as well, as long as you have some sincere motivation. But in the end, the Tibetan problem has to be solved between the Han Chinese and the Tibetans. No one else can do this for us.

We Tibetans extend our right hand to our Han Chinese friends and our left hand to our Western supporters. Of the two hands, the right hand is considered more important. We extend this hand to the Chinese government. But as long as this right hand remains empty, our left hand accepts help from other people who are really concerned for us. It is only logical and natural. When the right hand gets some concrete result, then the left hand will withdraw and wave goodbye.

It is extremely important that our Han Chinese brothers and sisters have full awareness of the Tibetan problem. It is helpful to take every opportunity to tell them about Tibetan culture, Tibetan language, or Tibetan spirituality. Then there will be a chance to say something about history, considering Tibetan views and Chinese views. Among the Chinese, there are different views about history; not everyone accepts the official version. We need a realistic approach and in order to have that, we need fuller knowledge about reality. Maybe some of you can help in this way.

Junior Students in the Dharma

According to the conventional understanding of history, the Buddha came to the world almost twenty-six hundred years ago. Eventually the teachings of the Buddha spread from India to different regions, including Southeast Asia and East Asia. Today, Burma, Sri Lanka, Thailand, Cambodia, and so forth mainly follow the Pali tradition. In China, Korea, Japan, Vietnam—as well as Tibet and Mongolia—the Pali tradition is present, but there is also the Sanskrit tradition.[13] For understanding Buddhism in the Sanskrit tradition, Chinese language is most important, followed by Tibetan. Buddhism flourished in China at least three or four centuries earlier than in Tibet.

I consider the Pali tradition to be the most senior; it is the foundation of the Buddha Dharma. Those who hold this tradition are the most senior students of the Buddha. Then, within the Sanskrit tradition, the Chinese Buddhists are the most senior Buddhists. We, the Tibetans and Mongolians, rank after that. So, whenever I give a teaching to the Chinese community, I always begin by expressing my respect to them as elder students of the Buddha.

At the same time, I might mention that as far as knowledge is concerned, junior students are sometimes better. Tibetan Buddhism was established by Shantarakshita, one of the very best logicians and philosophers of the Nalanda tradition. He personally came to Tibet. He and his student Kamalashila were both great scholars and their writings are still available. They were great logicians, Madhyamika philosophers and monks; naturally they wanted their students, the Tibetans, also to be like that. Even now, in the twenty-first century, we study important texts in a rigorous way. First, we memorize them and then get a word-by-word explanation. After that, we debate their meaning in a thorough and highly precise way. Tibetans in general have knowledge of the Buddha Dharma simply because of these great teachers; through them, we became real holders of the Nalanda tradition. So, in terms of having a deeper and more complete form of the teaching, I do think the Tibetan tradition is the best.

Between texts written by Indian masters and texts written by Tibetan masters, different circumstances led to different styles. India was not just Buddhist; there were many non-Buddhists and there were extensive discussions among the best scholars of the different traditions. So Indian masters like Nagarjuna and Aryadeva wrote texts that take a more comparative perspective and engage in deeper analysis. The Tibetan masters, on the other hand, took for granted that their audience was entirely Buddhist, so they do little comparison.

Reality Is neither Buddhist nor Christian

On this planet there are many different religious traditions; each started in a different area and each is suitable to the peoples of that region.

For more than one thousand years, and in some cases for more than two thousand years, these traditions have truly served humanity. Today, many millions of people get inspiration from these traditions. It is a fact. And in the future these major traditions will remain, serving humanity.

Sometimes in the past, the existence of many different religious traditions caused problems. From now on, I hope we will have fewer such problems because of a greater sense of closeness. We understand more about the value of other traditions. Just as there are many different kinds of people, there are different traditions that suit them. Generally speaking, in the West, Christianity is dominant; the culture has a Jewish and Christian heritage. It is often safer and better to keep to your own religious tradition.

To illustrate this, let me relate some things that I have personally observed. There was a Polish woman who was a Theosophist—I met her long ago at the Madras Theosophical Society.[14] After 1959, when a great many Tibetans came to India, she became very close with Tibetans and she helped many young Tibetan students with their education. As a result of this connection, she came to accept Buddhism as her own religion. But later, when she was more than eighty years old and approaching death, the concept of God as the Creator became more and more vivid in her mind. This certainly created some confusion for her.

Here is another story. There was a Tibetan woman who was married to a Tibetan government official. He died, leaving her with several small children. Christian missionaries helped her a great deal, making sure that the children were educated. In the mid-1960s, she came to see me and she was really very sad. Because the Christian missionaries had helped her so much, she had decided that *for this lifetime* she would be a Christian. But she resolved that in her next lifetime she would again be a Buddhist. Again, you can see that this is a clear sign of confusion.

These days, there are Westerners who have taken an interest in Buddhism and have become genuine Buddhist practitioners. But I must say that for the general public it is much better, and much safer, to stay with one's own tradition. By comparison, consider that there are millions of Tibetans and almost all of them are Buddhist—yet, in the Lhasa area over the last four centuries, some Tibetans have been Muslims. Generally, Muslims came from Ladakh, settled in Tibet, and married Tibetans. This caused no problem. Also, since the beginning of the twentieth century, there have been some very faithful Christian Tibetans; their numbers are quite small. Thus, out of six million Tibetans, a few thousand do find themselves more attracted to other traditions. Likewise, there are millions of Westerners whose heritage is basically Christian, but who have a special interest in Buddhism. In some cases, people want a kind of spirituality that they are not finding in their home tradition. If the Buddhist approach really helps you, then that is okay, but in any case it is extremely important always to keep genuine respect for your traditional religion.

Reality is neither Buddhist nor Christian. When I teach about Buddhism in the West, I always make this clear because I do feel some hesitancy.[15] On the other hand, when I teach Buddhism to Chinese, Tibetans, Mongolians, Japanese, or Vietnamese, I am aware that the majority of these peoples have traditionally been Buddhist. There is no problem. In fact, I have a sense that I am restoring to them their own traditional teachings, their Dharma, their religion.

I am especially moved, so very deeply touched, when I have the chance to give Buddhist teachings to Indian Buddhists. Everywhere in the world that I go to teach, my whole message is nothing but ancient Indian thought. That's all there is. For example, the message of nonviolence, *ahimsa*—this is the Indian tradition. And everything I am teaching here about the path to enlightenment—this is the treasure of the Nalanda tradition. When I teach my Indian friends, I think of how we kept alive in Tibet the treasure that they largely lost over the centuries. It gives me an incredible feeling of happiness to return this to them.

There is great value in maintaining your own tradition. Of course, you can include some practices from other traditions such as Buddhism. Some of my Christian friends are developing compassion, tolerance, and a sense of contentment by incorporating some Buddhist techniques—without changing religion. This seems healthy and good.

On the other hand, when my Christian friends are curious about emptiness, I usually laugh and tell them, "This is not your business." I am joking, but in a way I do want to caution them that their interest in emptiness may harm their faith in a Creator, in something absolute, in a powerful God. It is difficult to talk about such things from a Buddhist viewpoint.

Many years ago in England, a Christian group asked me to teach the Gospels to a Christian community. This was a big challenge because Buddhists, strictly speaking, do not believe in a divine Creator. So they were asking me to help to promote faith in a Creator in whom I myself do not believe. But I did my best. I used some of the reasons for belief found in ancient Indian traditions that do accept a Creator. The audience was very pleased by my explanation of some passages from the Gospels. In fact, I think they really did get a deeper understanding of God.

Of course these different religious traditions have tremendous philosophical differences, but they are the same at the practical level. They show us how to practice love, kindness—together with forgiveness, tolerance, self-discipline, and contentment. Along with faith, all major religions teach these things. One of my Christian friends in Australia, a minister who is very much involved in helping the poor, introduced me to an audience as "a good Christian." I really liked that. I joked with him, telling him that I consider him a good Buddhist. The point is that there are so many practices in common among traditions, and all of them are sincerely practiced with a sense of dedication to the well-being of others. That is the purpose.

When you practice with a sense of dedication to the well-being of others, then you yourself feel fulfilled. This is the purpose of our life. What is the point of having merely a luxurious way of life, spending lots of money, while on the same planet others are facing terrible difficulties, even starving? Helping others, serving others—this is the real meaning of life. And if you believe that God created us as social beings, then there must be some deep meaning in this. Among social animals, the very basis of life is taking care of each other, showing concern, helping one other.

Truly Practicing

Gung-tang Rinpoche's songs include these lines:[16]

> Having attained this precious human life of leisure and opportunity, there is a danger that I may lose it without giving it meaning. So now is the time for me to reach for liberation.

He goes on to admonish himself:

> Now, therefore, I must be seized—as though by an iron hook—by awareness of impermanence.

We all have to recognize the tremendous opportunity that we have. As humans we have this rare intelligence, but there is a real danger that we will waste it. Death is certain, but when we will die is totally unpredictable. We could lose our precious human existence at any moment. With such reflections, we must motivate ourselves to do something meaningful *right now*. The best way to make your human existence meaningful is to really engage in the practice of Dharma. During formal sitting meditation and in between sessions, in different ways, be mindful and introspectively vigilant. Keep constant watch on your mind.

Remember that such practices are common to all traditions. It is entirely up to individuals—whether they accept religion or not—to decide whether to do these practices. You do not have to be a religious person in order to be a good, sensitive human being; among nonbelievers, there are many wonderful people. But if you do accept religion, then you should be serious and sincere. Make the teachings of your tradition a real part of your life. Every day, from the moment you wake, use one corner of your mind to watch your mind and your behavior.

One time in Jerusalem, I was in a meeting with some Jews and Palestinians together. An Israeli Jewish teacher told us how he teaches his students to deal with situations where they cannot avoid people they do not like. For example, he said that his Palestinian students feel a sense of agitation at Israeli checkpoints. He advised his students that, when meeting someone whose presence agitates their minds, they should practice considering that person as someone made in God's image. His students told him that this was extremely helpful. When they remembered his advice, their minds were much calmer and it was easier to meet the guards at checkpoints without being overwhelmed with irritation. This is what practice means. We actually have to do these things. The whole point of religious teaching is its practical implementation, which can be so wonderful.

In order to carry out a practice—such as constantly watching the mind—you should form a determination, make a pledge, right when you wake up: "Now, for the rest of this day, I will put into practice what I believe just as much as I can." It is very important that, at the start of the day, we should set out to shape what will happen later. Then, at the end of every day, check what happened. Review the day. And if you carried through for that whole day your morning's determination, then rejoice. Reinforce further your motivation to continue in the same line. However, when you do your reviewing, you may discover that you did things during the day that are contrary to your religious values and beliefs. You should then acknowledge this and cultivate a deep sense of remorse. Strengthen your resolve not to indulge in these actions in the future.

If you keep practicing in this way, then it is certain that over time there will be real change, genuine transformation, within your mind. This is the way to improve. It is impossible to really change through one session of prayer. But improvement definitely can come by constantly watching our minds and carrying out the practices we believe in day-by-day, year-by-year, decade-by-decade. This understanding is common to believers of all religious traditions.

CHAPTER TWO

The Great Value of This Teaching

Transmission

THIS BOOK, the *Great Treatise on the Stages of the Path to Enlightenment*, was of course written by Atisha Dipamkara, an eleventh-century Bengali who came to Tibet.[17] Shantarakshita had come in the eighth century, so by the eleventh century the Nalanda tradition was well established in Tibet. Atisha composed a short text, *Lamp for the Path to Enlightenment*, with the aim of providing a way to integrate the various Buddhist teachings intended for practitioners at different levels of mental capacity.[18] Atisha's *Lamp* became the root of all stages of the path (*lam rim*) literature. In that sense, one can treat Tsong-kha-pa 's *Great Treatise on the Stages of the Path to Enlightenment* as an extensive commentary on, or exposition of, that short text by Atisha.

I received the transmission of these teachings on the *Great Treatise* from Trijang Rinpoche and from Ling Rinpoche, my two tutors. Trijang Rinpoche had received these teachings from his teacher, Pabongka Rinpoche. Ling Rinpoche also had Pabongka in his lineage, but in addition—when he was quite young—he also received these teachings from the Thirteenth Dalai Lama.

The Buddha

The *Great Treatise* (1: 33) opens with a salutation to Manjushri[19] in the Sanskrit language. This is partly to indicate that the source of the Tibetan tradition is the Sanskrit tradition. Sanskrit became the dominant medium through which the Buddha's teaching was presented in the Nalanda tradition. The custom evolved to acknowledge that the teaching derives from Indian sources by often placing a salutation in Sanskrit at the beginning of Tibetan texts.

Then, in Tibetan, the text opens with a salutation to the Buddha. Here Tsong-kha-pa pays homage to the Buddha by reflecting upon the qualities of the Buddha's body, speech, and mind. In the first line he reflects upon the qualities of the Buddha's body, pointing out that the Buddha's physical body came into being as a result of its causes. This is an important idea, right here. The Buddha's embodiment in form results from specific causes and Tsong-kha-pa identifies those causes as good qualities—by which he means virtuous acts. Even the attainment of buddhahood is the result of something; it arises from causes and conditions. Buddhahood does not come out of nowhere, nor is it an eternal permanent state that is uncaused. In a sense, Tsong-kha-pa is echoing the point Dignaga makes in the opening stanza of his *Compendium of Valid Cognition* where, in identifying Buddha as a reliable person, he says that the Buddha has *become* such a person.[20] Commenting on that, Dharmakirti says that in order to negate the idea that the Buddha was uncaused, Dignaga intentionally uses the term "become."[21] The Buddha, through some processes, *came to be* a reliable person.

Tsong-kha-pa speaks about the Buddha's body as arising from a vast array of causes. These causes are listed in various texts, particularly in studies of the Perfection of Wisdom tradition, but they are also explicitly mentioned in Nagarjuna's *Precious Garland.*[22] Tsong-kha-pa emphasizes that even the Buddha whom we revere, the Blessed Buddha, was previously an ordinary being on the path to becoming a buddha. There was a time when the Buddha was just like us. By gathering all of the relevant conditions, he evolved into a fully enlightened being.

To understand fully the significance of this first line—that the Buddha's body is born of a vast array of excellent causes—you have to understand the relationships among the four noble truths.[23] And in order to understand completely the presentation of the four noble truths, you have to develop an understanding of the teaching of the two truths, the conventional and the ultimate.[24] In particular, it is important for you to understand how the two truths have the same nature but distinct identities. We will explain more when we discuss the practices pertaining to the person of medium capacity.[25] Implicit in this line on how the Buddha's qualities are born from a vast array of excellent causes is the important principle of dependent origination in terms of cause and effect.

Tsong-kha-pa writes that the Buddha's *speech* fulfills the hopes and aspirations of countless sentient beings, limitless living beings. The "hopes" of countless beings means their welfare. The welfare of living beings includes their immediate and temporary welfare as well as their long-term, ultimate welfare. To be able to fulfill their welfare in either sense, the Buddha needs a deep understanding of what these needs are and how most effectively to meet them. The primary way that the Buddha acts for the welfare of others is speech. Thus, the enlightened quality of the Buddha's speech is its capacity to fulfill the aspirations of living beings.

In some texts we find reference to the Buddha's qualities in terms of their supernormal nature; there are marvelous qualities associated with the Buddha's body, speech, and mind. Various texts identify marvelous qualities of the Buddha's physical *body*; the marvelous quality of the Buddha's *mind* is that it can realize all facts. The Buddha's speech is marvelous in providing instructions that help all beings. Of these three, the qualities of the Buddha's speech are always considered the most important.

In his *Praise to the Buddha for Teaching Dependent Origination* Tsong-kha-pa writes—addressing the Buddha—that among all of your enlightened activities the most important is your speech and that, within that, speech teaching dependent origination is the very most important.[26] Also, in Nagarjuna's texts, his opening salutations to the Buddha often involve particularly recognizing the Buddha's having taught dependent origination.[27]

We notice that Tsong-kha-pa identifies the qualities of the Buddha's body primarily from the point of view of its *causes*. Then, when identifying the qualities of the Buddha's speech, he does this mainly in terms of its *results*, how it brings about the welfare of others. And when identifying the qualities of the Buddha's mind, he identifies the enlightened quality of the Buddha's mind as its capacity to be fully immersed in realization of ultimate truth while in the same instant perceiving the world of diversity as well. This enlightened mind of the Buddha is the actual identity of buddhahood. So he praises the Buddha's mind from the perspective of its being the *nature* of buddhahood.

After paying homage to the Buddha as the great sage of the Shakya clan, in subsequent stanzas Tsong-kha-pa makes salutations to Manjushri and Maitreya[28] and then to Nagarjuna and Asanga, the two main pioneers of the Mahayana tradition. He then also makes salutations to Atisha Dipamkara, who is, in a sense, the founder of this lineage of teachings on the stages of the path, and also to the great masters who are upholders of this lineage.

Integrated Practice

Tsong-kha-pa (1: 33) then explains his primary motivation for composing the *Great Treatise*. This is quite important. He says that he sees many people who are deeply dedicated to meditation, but are lacking in learning. Because of this deficiency, they focus on just one or two aspects of a particular practice. With only minimal understanding of the overall Buddhist path, they cannot take an approach that integrates into practice all the key elements of the essential teachings.

Those who are learned can sometimes be very skilled at integrating the teachings into their personal practice. But in other cases those who are highly learned in Buddhist text-traditions do not seem to have much actual experience. They may get very little benefit from all of their Dharma learning. Today, we see cases where learning seems to serve as a further reinforcement for the scholar's ego, creating conceit, jealousy, and other problems. Even when these negative qualities are not pronounced, some teachers somehow seem lost when it comes to applying what they know in practice. Faced with the vast dimensions of the teachings, their approach is scattered. Such scholars are somehow unable to bring the teachings together in an integrated format that is useful for actual practice.

Furthermore, Tsong-kha-pa says that many individuals show partiality in their study and in their practice. For example, in Tibet, when someone happens to be keen in the practice of the Sutra path, then they tend to ignore the Vajrayana teachings.[29] If someone happens to be a practitioner of Vajrayana, then they tend to ignore the Sutra teachings. If someone is enthusiastic about epistemological studies, then they may specialize in just that. For others, it may be Abhidharma or monastic discipline.

So there are meditation practitioners with no learning, scholars of great learning who cannot apply their learning to practice, and also many others who are in various ways one-sided in their approach to study and practice. Tsong-kha-pa says that all three of these are cases of being unable to practice the Dharma in a way that would truly please those who have wisdom. He means that none of these persons can practice on the basis of an integrated approach encompassing all essential elements of the Buddhist path.

What Atisha gave us in his *Lamp for the Path to Enlightenment* was just such a way to integrate all of the key elements of the Dharma for an individual practitioner, one person sitting on one cushion. So Tsong-kha-pa says that his heart takes great delight in writing an extensive exposition of Atisha's *Lamp* because it offers a way to practice that *will* please those who have great wisdom. It brings all of the key elements of the teaching into a framework within which one person can practice them all *in stages*.

This integration is very similar to what Aryadeva presents in his *Four Hundred Stanzas on the Middle Way*; there we also have a series of stages. On the first level, you must avoid nonvirtuous actions; in the middle stage, you must stop grasping at self; and finally, you must stop grasping at all views. The one who fully understands this approach is truly wise.[30]

Listen Well

In the final stanza of his salutation Tsong-kha-pa (1: 34) calls upon readers who may benefit from this approach, asking them to listen well. Such readers will be those with minds unclouded by biased thinking, the mental capacity to distinguish right from wrong, and an interest in finding real meaning in their human existence of leisure and opportunity. He asks those of us with such good fortune, "Please listen to what I have to say with a single-pointed mind."

Again, this is strikingly similar to Aryadeva's *Four Hundred*, which says that a practitioner of the Dharma who is listening to the teachings needs three qualities: objectivity, critical intelligence, and a real interest in what is being taught.[31]

Atisha and the Stages of the Path Tradition

Tsong-kha-pa (1: 35-43) then explains the greatness of the text's author, by which he means the Indian master Atisha. Atisha's teaching derives from two primary lineages. One stems from Nagarjuna and pertains mainly to the Buddha's teaching on the philosophical *view* of emptiness, emphasizing dependent origination and its relation to ultimate reality. The other is Maitreya's lineage, passed through Asanga to successive masters. Here the primary focus is the *method* aspect of the Mahayana path, especially practices involving the cultivation of loving-kindness, compassion, and the spirit of enlightenment (*bodhichitta*). These two lineages really converge in Atisha.

In Tibet, Atisha's teachings evolved in three main lines. One was the "Kadam great text" lineage of Potowa,[32] which understands Atisha's instructions on the basis of study and practice of six principal Indian texts. The first two of these texts are the *Jataka Tales*, stories of the Buddha's past lives, and the *Collection of Aphorisms*.[33] These two texts are seen mainly as a basis for cultivating and enhancing your devotion to the Buddha. Then, Asanga's *Bodhisattva Levels* and Maitreya's *Orna-*

ment for the Mahayana Sutras are considered mainly in terms of teachings on meditative states; they deal extensively with the various levels and paths in Mahayana practice.[34] And the last two texts are Shantideva's *Compendium of Instructions* and his *Engaging in the Bodhisattva Deeds*, presenting primarily the bodhisattva's practices.[35]

A second lineage—the "Kadam stages of the path" lineage—evolved among Atisha's students who based practice on texts presenting the stages of the path (*lam rim*) or stages of the teaching (*den rim*). And there also evolved a third lineage, the "Kadam personal instructions" lineage, emphasizing small, personal instruction texts designed for specific situations.

When you approach stages of the path teachings, including Tsong-kha-pa's *Great Treatise*, you can find all three of these lineages. Tsong-kha-pa received the teachings of all three. Moreover, if you look at the *Great Treatise*, most of its source texts are really in the Perfection of Wisdom literature. In fact, Tsong-kha-pa's student Gyel-tsap wrote a book on the Perfection of Wisdom literature in which he sometimes cites the *Great Treatise*, thus showing this close connection.[36]

You are primarily following the approach of the "*lam rim* great texts" lineage if you study the *Great Treatise* on the basis of its seven supporting texts— Tsong-kha-pa's *Ocean of Reasoning*, *Illumination of the Thought*, *Essence of Eloquence*, the insight sections of his *Great Treatise* and *Shorter Treatise*, and his *Golden Garland of Eloquence*, as well as Gyel-tsap's *Heart Ornament of Explanation*. Or you can instead follow the "Kadam stages of the path" lineage by concentrating mainly on Tsong-kha-pa's *Great Treatise* and *Shorter Treatise*. However, Tsong-kha-pa stated that, since there are hardly any people who know how to apply in practice all of these explanations, more condensed versions for practice should be made. So his followers composed many instructional texts on the stages of the path, both in brief and in detail. There are the six shorter texts in the famous collection of eight great guides to the stages of the path, but there are also many other texts of that sort.[37] If your approach follows these texts, then you are following the "*lam rim* personal instructions" lineage. So within the context of the study and practice of the stages of the path, you can follow three different lineages deriving from Atisha's followers.

Atisha and the Four Schools of Tibetan Buddhism

Following Atisha's arrival in Tibet and composition of the *Lamp for the Path to Enlightenment*, each of the four main schools of Tibetan Buddhism in some way adopted the pattern and structure of the stages of the path teachings. For example, in the Nyingma tradition, Long-chenpa's *Mind at Ease* presents the path in a way that follows the basic structure of Atisha's approach.[38] The same is true of Sakya Pandita's *Clear Elucidation of the Buddha's Intent,* which could be seen as a fusion of the stages of the path teachings with mind training (*lojong)* teachings.[39] Similarly, in the Kagyu tradition, Gampopa's *Jewel Ornament of Liberation* presents the basic structure of the path in a manner just like what Atisha lays out.[40] Sometimes slightly different sequences are adopted, but basically in all of these traditions the stages of the path are very similar. For example, the *Jewel Ornament of Liberation* speaks of turning one's mind away from four things. If you look at these four turnings of mind, they echo teachings in the stages of the path tradition.[41]

Two Aspirations

In a sense, Atisha's teachings derive from a point that Nagarjuna makes in his *Precious Garland.*[42] Nagarjuna explains that if you examine all the teachings of the Buddha, they can be classified into two categories related to two aspirations: (1) aspiration to attain a fortunate rebirth in a higher realm and (2) aspiration to obtain ultimate liberation or, as Nagarjuna calls it, "definite goodness." All of the teachings of the Buddha, in one way or another, relate to the fulfillment of these two aspirations.

How do we fulfill our aspirations for better rebirth? This is done through adopting a way of life that is not harming, nonviolent. The heart of that practice is to live one's life on the basis of trust and confidence in the law of karma. So it requires cultivation of confidence that dependent arising works in the sense that our actions have karmic effects. Living one's life according to that conviction is the primary method by which one seeks to fulfill the aspiration to gain a fortunate rebirth.

The other aspiration is to seek final enlightenment or liberation, and here the primary method is to cultivate an understanding of the ultimate nature of reality. We understand the ultimate nature of reality primarily through the Buddha's teaching that dependent arising entails emptiness. One needs to cultivate wisdom. Thus, the key factors one needs to cultivate in Buddhist practice—confidence in karma and wisdom knowing emptiness—both derive from understanding dependent arising.

Attainment of liberation can be in two forms. One is the liberation of individuals, liberation from unenlightened existence. But there is also attainment of buddhahood for the benefit of all beings. Earlier we saw that the primary quality of the Buddha's speech is its ability to fulfill the aspirations of all beings. This is the aim of the Mahayana practitioner, a person motivated to bring about the welfare of all beings. The welfare of all beings is the purpose for which the Mahayana practitioner seeks to attain buddhahood. Because of that motivation, she or he needs to complement the path of wisdom with *bodhichitta*, the spirit of enlightenment. These two together will allow one to bring about realization of that final aspiration.

Among the six texts that Atisha's followers used to practice the stages of the path in the Kadam great text lineage of Potowa, the *Jataka Tales* and the *Collection of Aphorisms* primarily pertain to developing confidence in karma, Asanga's *Bodhisattva Levels* and Maitreya's *Ornament for the Mahayana Sutras* can be understood as pertaining to the compassionate motivation of Mahayana practitioners, and Shantideva's *Compendium of Instructions* and his *Engaging in the Bodhisattva Deeds* can be understood as pertaining to the view of emptiness. I find this perspective on the six texts most helpful.

There Are No Contradictions in the Buddha's Teaching

What we have discussed so far gives us a sense of the greatness of the stages of the path teaching by highlighting the authenticity of its origins and sources. Another way to inspire confidence in the teaching is to explain the greatness of the teaching itself. One of the reasons Atisha's teaching on stages of the path is great is that it allows an individual practitioner to realize that there are no contradictions among all the teachings of the Buddha (1: 46-49).

The Buddha's speech has the capacity to fulfill the diverse aspirations of countless beings. So the beings who are helped by the Buddha's speech are not just limitless in *number*. They are also limitless in the *diversity* of their mental dispositions as individuals. To accommodate the diversity of mental dispositions and mental levels among his audience, the Buddha gave many different teachings. Depending upon the level of one's aspiration, one can distinguish those of the Mahayana from those of the Fundamental Vehicle. Also, one can distinguish the four classical Buddhist schools of India according to the level of understanding of the wisdom teachings.[43] If you simply take these different teachings as individual texts, then on the surface they seem to contradict one another. However, Atisha's stages of the path approach allows you to understand this diversity not only as an accommodation to different individuals, but also as useful to a single practitioner as he or she progresses to different levels of realization.

For example, among the teachings on wisdom there are different levels of subtlety in the explanation of selflessness. If we relate these teachings to our own mental states, how we perceive the world, then we can see that each of them may be highly effective in particular situations. When we observe our minds and consider how we imagine our own identity, we recognize that we often see ourselves as possessing some kind of unitary, eternal, autonomous reality—something internal that we call "self" or "soul." We grasp on to this. The Buddha's teachings refuting such a self are then immediately applicable, helping us to dissolve that kind of grasping.

Likewise, when we examine how we relate to the *external* world, we recognize that we act as though the physical world out there had some kind of independent reality of its own. It seems to possess some distinct reality completely independent of our perceptions. In this case, the Buddha's Chittamatra teaching—rejecting an external, objective world—helps us to dissolve that kind of grasping.

Thus, many of the teachings seem contradictory on the surface but make sense in relation to the needs of an individual who is progressing in realization and dealing with a series of different mental distortions. Atisha's teaching on the stages of the path shows us that all the Buddha's teachings are useful to a single individual, without any contradiction.

Taking All the Teachings as Personal Instructions

Tsong-kha-pa (1: 50-53) explains that another benefit of the stages of the path teaching is that it allows you to understand all the teachings of the Buddha as personal instructions. Some people adopt the perspective that among Buddhist teachings there are two fundamentally different categories: (1) the class of scholastic texts that are really relevant only for expanding your knowledge and (2) other teachings that are relevant for your personal practice. Tsong-kha-pa considers this dichotomy to be mistaken and unhelpful.

If you adopt Atisha's approach, then you see that all Buddhist teachings have direct relevance to your own personal practice. They are all personal instructions because there is nothing in the teachings of the Buddha that is not related, in one way or another, to training and taming your own mind and heart.

The Ultimate Intention of the Buddha's Teachings

Another benefit of the stages of the path approach is that it allows you to understand the ultimate intention of the Buddha's teachings (1: 53). The ultimate intention of the Buddha's teachings is to give us the means to fulfill our aspirations to attain a fortunate rebirth and to attain final liberation. The stages of the path teachings allow us to see all Buddhist teachings as contributing, in one way or another, to the fulfillment of these two aspirations.

Avoiding the Error of Rejecting Buddhist Teachings

Tsong-kha-pa (1: 53-54) identifies the final greatness of the stages of the path approach as its preventing the grave error of rejecting the Buddha's teachings, rejecting the Dharma. Here Tsong-kha-pa cites many texts, including the Perfection of Wisdom sutras, where the Buddha states that a practitioner must study, understand, and actually practice all aspects of the path. If you really aspire to help many billions of living beings with diverse mental dispositions, then you have to understand and practice many diverse teachings and approaches. This is what prepares you.

Historically, it has been a tradition among Tibetan masters to study and also to practice all the lineages—Sakya, Kagyu, Geluk, Nyingma—and Jonang as well.[44] This is an excellent model. We should adopt a *nonsectarian* approach, not just studying all of these lineages but also putting their teachings into practice.

A Question about Shugden

Question: Your Holiness, I feel agitated to see and hear the Shugden protesters outside the building here.[45] How do I help myself? Please address this issue, as many are misinformed about this.

Answer: We have had this problem for 370 years. It started during the time of the Fifth Dalai Lama. And from 1951 until the 1970s, I myself worshipped this spirit. I used to be one of the practitioners!

One of my reasons for abandoning Shugden worship is that much of my efforts are directed to promoting nonsectarianism—especially *within* Tibetan Buddhism. I always encourage people to receive teachings from the teachers of diverse traditions. This is like the Fifth Dalai

Lama, and many other great lamas, who received teachings within many traditions. Since the late 1960s and early 1970s, down to today, I have been practicing this way myself.

A Nyingma teacher, Kunu Lama Rinpoche, initially gave me teachings on Shantideva's texts. This lama was very nonsectarian, having received innumerable teachings from many different traditions. After that, I wanted to receive from this great lama a certain teaching distinct to the Nyingma tradition. I asked my tutor, Ling Rinpoche, pointing out that I had already received some teachings from this lama, but I now wanted to receive teachings on an important Nyingma tantric text.

Ling Rinpoche was a little bit cautious about this because of Shugden. He never worshipped the spirit, but he was cautious about it. (My other tutor, Trijang Rinpoche, was very close to this spirit practice.) The rumor that was circulating was that if a Geluk lama takes teachings in the Nyingma tradition, Shugden would destroy him. Ling Rinpoche was a bit frightened for me and he really warned me to be careful. The Shugden worshippers have a tradition that one must be extremely strict about one's own distinctive Geluk tradition.

Actually, I think this standpoint deprives people of religious freedom, preventing them from taking other teachings. In practice, discouraging a standpoint that deprives people of the freedom to choose is actually an affirmation of religious freedom. A double negation is an affirmation.

Around 1970, I was reading the life stories of many great lamas, mainly of the Geluk tradition. I had the idea that if Shugden is truly reliable, then most of the great lamas who tutored the Dalai Lamas must have practiced Shugden worship. It turns out that this is not the case. So I developed some doubt and the more I investigated, the clearer it became.

For example, the Fifth Dalai Lama very explicitly explains his position vis-à-vis the worship of this spirit.[46] He explains what it is and he explains the causes and conditions that gave rise to it. He describes the destructive functions of this particular spirit. He says that it arose from misguided motivation and that as a spirit it manifests as a violator of a pledge. According to the Fifth Dalai Lama, its function is to harm both the Buddhist doctrine and living beings.

Once I realized these things, it was my moral responsibility to make the facts clear. Whether you listen to me is entirely up to you as an individual. From the outset, I told both Tibetans and some of our other friends what I had come to understand. They are free to listen to my advice or not. It is an individual right to accept religion or not to accept it. Accepting this religion or that religion is entirely up to the individual.

My opinion is that Shugden worship is actually not a genuine practice of Dharma; it is simply worship of a worldly spirit. This is another aspect of the problem: from what I have taught, I think you can see that Tibetan Buddhism is a continuation of the pure lineage of the Nalanda tradition, which relies on reasoning, not blind belief. So it is very sad that certain Tibetan practices could cause this profound and rich tradition to become a sort of spirit worship.

Both the Fifth Dalai Lama and the Thirteenth Dalai Lama were gravely critical toward this spirit. Since I am considered the reincarnation of these Dalai Lamas, it is only logical that my life should follow theirs. One could say that it proves that I am a true reincarnation!

It seems that these people outside are really fond of worshipping this spirit. Okay, it is their life; I have no problem if that is what they want to do. When I taught in Germany a group of Shugden followers shouted for at least three or four hours. Eventually I felt great concern about how their throats would be affected by so much shouting.

CHAPTER THREE

The Heart of Buddhism

Wisdom Changes Our Minds

SOME SCHOLARS SAY that Buddhism is not a religion, but a science of mind.[47] There is a sense in which this is true because for Buddhism—and other nontheistic religions—the core concept is causality. Effects arise from causes, again and again. We are very much concerned with suffering, pain, on the one hand, and on the other, what is joyful or pleasant, a sense of great happiness. Pains and pleasures are feelings. And feelings are part of our mind. While there are external causes as well, the *main* causes of such feelings are right here within our own minds. It logically follows that the reduction of suffering, pain, worry, sadness, and fear ultimately depends upon our mental attitude.

All Buddhist teachings are based on the four noble truths. Within the teaching of the four noble truths we recognize two sets of cause and effect. One set relates to the nature of suffering—which we do not naturally desire—and its origin. This pair pertains to the class of afflicted phenomena, to unenlightened existence. The second cause and effect pair relates to happiness—what we aspire for and we wish to achieve—and its causes. These belong to the class of enlightened phenomena.

Aspiration is important, but in itself cannot bring about the profound transformation we are seeking. In seeking to reshape our minds, having only a wish for things to be different will help in a very limited way. To bring about profound change we need very firm conviction. Deep and firm conviction must come out of analytical meditation in which we see for ourselves how things are. Therefore, the Buddhist approach is to use human intelligence to the greatest possible extent, thereby bringing about a transformation of our minds.

At the beginning of the *Heart Sutra,* the Buddha Shakyamuni remains in meditation during a dialogue between Shariputra and Avalokiteshvara.[48] Shariputra asks, "If a bodhisattva wishes to engage in the practices of the perfection of wisdom, how shall he go about it?" Avalokiteshvara answers that the bodhisattva who wishes to engage in the practices of the perfection of wisdom must view all five aggregates—the physical and the mental aggregates—to be devoid of inherent existence. Right from the outset, the *Heart Sutra* indicates the need for cultivation of the wisdom knowing emptiness. Determination to change your mind motivates practice, but it is determination complemented with the faculty of wisdom that will make the real difference. Therefore, between the two main ways of approaching the path—an approach formed by aspiration and determination and one formed through the application of wisdom—the latter is more important.

What is wisdom? Sometimes wisdom pertains to the conventional level and sometimes it pertains to the ultimate truth. Of these two, wisdom knowing the ultimate truth is the primary meaning. Thus, when we speak of the perfection of wisdom, as in the Perfection of Wisdom texts, we are not talking about just any wisdom. We mean a wisdom knowing that things are empty of inherent existence, and we mean that type of wisdom when it is developed to the level of a perfect virtue. To be a *perfection* of wisdom, the wisdom knowing emptiness must be reinforced and complemented by the spirit of enlightenment, *bodhichitta.*[49]

Wisdom that directly knows emptiness and is complemented with the spirit of enlightenment—this is the perfection of wisdom, which in Sanskrit is *prajna-paramita. Prajna* is "wisdom" and *paramita* means "to go beyond." This etymology points at an actual process of going beyond where we are now. It suggests that there is something to which we can go that is far beyond where we are now. Wisdom directly knowing emptiness, when present in a bodhisattva's mental stream—this is the perfection of wisdom. Particularly in the Sanskrit Buddhist tradition, wisdom is critical.

Conditions for Learning

After explaining the greatness of the author (Atisha) and of the stages of the path teaching itself, Tsong-kha-pa (1: 55-67) discusses how to teach and to listen to the Dharma. With what kind of attitudes and states of mind do we do this?

We teach and we listen to the teachings in order to fulfill our immediate welfare and our long-term welfare. Both the listener and the teacher need to meet certain conditions so that what is taught and what is heard will really become as beneficial and as effective as possible. As a listener, in order to benefit from the teachings, you need conditions that allow your state of mind, your attitude, and your motivation for listening to remain pure.

It is also important that the teacher's motivation for giving the teachings be unadulterated, pure. The teacher's motivation must be to benefit the students who are listening. Many qualities of a good teacher have been identified (1: 70-75), including the four qualities for attracting students (2: 225).[50] Among these four, the last two are very important: (1) teaching appropriately and (2) living by the ideals that you teach, making your own life an example. The teacher has to have the skill to adapt the teachings according to the level, the need, and specific circumstances of the listeners so that it is most effective in bringing about the necessary transformation. When these conditions are created, then it will be most beneficial to teach or to listen to Dharma teachings.

How to Guide Students

There are many different approaches to guiding students in the actual instructions of the Buddha Shakyamuni (1: 69). Even within Nagarjuna's writings, we see different approaches. In his *Precious Garland* he first presents all the teachings pertaining to the attainment of a fortunate rebirth. He explains the teaching on the ethical discipline of adopting virtue and abstaining from ten nonvirtuous actions.[51] He explains how to live without falling prey to various forms of wrong livelihood. Then, in the second part of the *Precious Garland*, Nagarjuna explains practices related to the attainment of liberation, nirvana, which he calls "definite goodness." In that context, he explains the correct view of emptiness. This approach makes sense because the *Precious Garland* is explicitly written as a letter of advice to a king. The teachings are presented as instructions tailored to a particular individual.

In Nagarjuna's *Essay on the Spirit of Enlightenment*, he takes a very different approach.[52] The entirety of the *Essay on the Spirit of Enlightenment* is an exposition of a stanza from the root tantra of *Guhyasamaja*, where it explains how all phenomena are devoid of intrinsic existence, devoid of the duality of subject and object. It explains equanimity in terms of the lack of inherent existence in all phenomena. Since this is presented as a commentary on *Guhyasamaja*, clearly Nagarjuna's audience is advanced practitioners, people who practice highest yoga tantra. Naturally, the procedure for presenting the path to people who are training in highest yoga tantra is different. Nagarjuna begins with an immediate explanation of emptiness and how to develop the correct view of ultimate reality. First, one studies teachings on emptiness and develops a deep understanding. Through analytical reflection upon this understanding, one reaches a deep ascertainment of the meaning of emptiness. Internalizing this in meditation, the practitioner eventually arrives at a point where there is a distinctive experiential flavor. With that kind of personal knowledge of emptiness, it becomes clear that it really is possible to end suffering. You know that suffering arises from ignorance, a distorted mental state, and you know that there is a powerful antidote to that mental state. There is a wisdom that directly negates the content of the deluded perspective of that ignorant mind. By seeing that you really can negate the root of suffering, you recognize that it is truly possible to end suffering.

Knowing that it is actually possible to end suffering can lead to a powerful feeling of compassion for all beings. Therefore, after explaining emptiness in his *Essay on the Spirit of Enlightenment*, Nagarjuna says, "In the person in whom the realization of emptiness has arisen, there is no doubt that attachment for all beings will arise."[53] Here the word "attachment" (*zhen pa*) refers to compassion.[54] Thus, the *Essay on the Spirit of Enlightenment* gives us a procedure where the practitioner begins by cultivating an understanding of emptiness—the ultimate spirit of enlightenment—and then on that basis cultivates the conventional spirit of enlightenment (*bodhichitta*).

These two approaches—that of the *Precious Garland* and that of the *Essay on the Spirit of Enlightenment*—are very different. A latter-day Tibetan master, Nyen-tsun Sung-rab, distinguishes approaches that are *specific to an individual* and *approaches that take into account the overall structure of the path*.[55] You can see that this idea applies to the quite different approaches found within Nagarjuna's teaching.

In short, when Tsong-kha-pa talks about how to guide the student on the basis of instructions, he means the Buddha's instructions. The purpose of the Buddha's instructions is to bring about the attainment of definite goodness, which is liberation and buddhahood. The principal factor needed to do this is wisdom.

Understanding Emptiness Is the Key

One can teach in a way tailored to a specific individual's need and situation or else one can teach with reference to the overall presentation of the Dharma. In his *Four Hundred* Aryadeva talks about two primary purposes in the Buddha's teachings.[56] One purpose is to realize our short-term aspiration to attain a favorable rebirth and the other is to attain liberation. Practices that are related to the attainment of a favorable rebirth mainly involve understanding the law of causality and the teaching on dependent origination in terms of karma. Yet when it comes to the presentation of karma, there are many aspects of how karma works that remain totally obscure to us. So at the outset we cultivate conviction in certain aspects of karmic cause-and-effect mainly through having admiration for our Teacher, the Buddha, and gaining some conviction or confidence based upon that admiration. But how do we get that kind of conviction?

The most skillful approach is to first understand the Buddha's teaching on emptiness, the teaching on selflessness. Dharmakirti's *Commentary on the Compendium of Valid Cognition* says that because the Buddha has proven to be faultless and fully reliable in important teachings such as the four noble truths, selflessness, and emptiness, we can extend the same level of conviction and confidence to other teachings that he gave.[57]

Thus, when it comes to teaching in terms of the overall presentation of the Dharma, the most important thing is to get a deeper understanding of the core teachings of the Buddha—the four noble truths, selflessness, and emptiness. Even among the four noble truths, the key point is to really develop a deep understanding of the third noble truth, the truth of cessation. We must recognize and really appreciate the possibility of attaining cessation. If we just look at the teachings on suffering and its origin without considering the end to suffering, then there is simply no point. Any deeper contemplation of suffering and its origin will just result in depression. And clearly the Buddha was not interested in merely making his followers depressed by having them delve ever deeper into the pervasiveness of suffering.

Suffering includes obvious suffering—physical pain and mental anguish—that we can all identify as such. But it also includes the suffering of change—something that we ordinarily identify as pleasurable experience, but which is unsatisfactory due to its changing, disintegrating, moment by moment. Then, there is the third level of suffering, the suffering of conditioning. Contemplating the nature of suffering, one comes to recognize that suffering—especially the suffering of conditioning, the most profound level of suffering—arises on the basis of karma and afflictions that are all rooted in fundamental ignorance, a mind grasping at some form of enduring self.

Once you recognize the distorted nature of that grasping, then you will appreciate the possibility of developing a perspective that directly opposes it. This allows you to recognize that there is at least a possibility of bringing an end to suffering. And once you recognize that, then there is real meaning and purpose to the contemplation of the first noble truth. Confidence in the Buddha's teachings on suffering and its origins rises from an appreciation of the Buddha's realization of the truth of cessation. Thus, when we really understand the Dharma, we see how all of the teachings are connected to the principal teaching on emptiness.

The purpose of the teaching of emptiness is the attainment of liberation.[58] If we confine our understanding of the Dharma to individual practices—such as guru yoga, reliance on the spiritual teacher, awareness of death and impermanence, taking refuge in the three jewels, or following the precepts—then we are not seeing these within the context of their deeper purpose—a purpose quite specific to Buddhism.

In fact, taking refuge, following precepts based upon that refuge, and many similar practices can be found in non-Buddhist teachings as well. Both in classical non-Buddhist teachings and in all contemporary non-Buddhist religious traditions you can find these in some form. They all have some version of taking refuge, they all have a notion living one's life according to precepts based on that refuge, and they all have some recognition of the importance of awareness of death. Also, when we look at ethical practices such as abstaining from killing, these need not be Buddhist practices. A non-Buddhist religious practitioner can abstain from killing based on the view that killing would violate God's wishes. One can even be totally nonreligious and abstain from killing out of fear of legal consequences. In that case, abstention from killing is not a religious practice at all.

Individual practices, when not tied to the ultimate aim of the Buddhist path, are not in themselves uniquely Buddhist. They are practices we have in common with all other traditions. For example, within the ethical discipline of abstaining from the ten nonvirtuous actions (1: 216-227), three are mental: abstaining from covetousness, malice, and wrong views. This is explained at the level of the practices relevant to the person of small capacity. Thus, the three poisons—attachment, aversion, and ignorance—are not listed, but rather very specific forms of these three are listed. Instead of the general category "attachment," we have a more specific form, covetousness; instead of aversion as a general category, we have malice. And for a person of small capacity, wrong views need not refer to wrong views about something profound. It can mean defying morality, killing with the thought that there will be no consequences. That kind of view is a wrong view.

You can see that such ethical practices are not distinctively Buddhist. What makes a particular practice uniquely Buddhist is its connection to a motivation to attain liberation. This purpose derives from understanding the truth of cessation, recognizing that it is possible to end suffering and the origin of suffering. Liberation (*moksha*)—or nirvana—does not mean transcending this world into some other plane, like a heavenly realm. Rather, it is a quality of the mental state of a person who has cleansed away stains of grasping at inherent existence or true existence. Thus, when a religious practice is complemented with an understanding of the Buddha's teaching on selflessness and emptiness, then it becomes a distinctly Buddhist practice. This is the point I want to make: studying the teaching on selflessness and developing the view of selflessness is really what constitutes any spiritual practice as *Buddhist*.

Questions for the Dalai Lama

Question: How do you define true happiness?

Answer: In Buddhism, happiness is not just a positive feeling but also a state of true freedom from suffering and its causes. It is a happiness that is lasting and deep.

In general, happiness means deep satisfaction. Sometimes even physical hardships, some types of physical suffering, can bring a sense of satisfaction. Between physical satisfaction and mental satisfaction, happiness mainly refers to mental satisfaction.

Sometimes ignorance gives rise to temporary mental satisfaction, a shortsighted kind of satisfaction. So to refine our definition, we could say that happiness is deep mental satisfaction that arises from awareness, from wisdom.

Question: If suffering is caused by the mind, what is one to do in difficult situations where *external* circumstances are hard to change? For example, if a spouse or father is an alcoholic, should the partner or the child stay and seek happiness there despite the partner's drinking? Or should one take the children and seek life without the drinker?

Answer: To say that suffering is caused by the mind per se is too general because even the Buddha has consciousness or mind. So the cause of suffering is not just the mind per se. It is an undisciplined, untamed mind.

Of course, there are always some conditions which are external and some conditions which are internal. In each situation, as it arises, one has to consider: In light of all of these conditions, what is the best course of action?

Question: Your Holiness, how is it possible to live an ordinary life—working at a job, paying bills, taking care of a family, and so on—without grasping?

Answer: How do you understand the idea of grasping? If your engagement with others is tainted by strong attachment, craving, aversion, anger, and so forth, then that form of grasping is undesirable. But on the other hand, when you are interacting with other living beings and become aware of their needs or suffering or pain, then you need to fully engage with that and be compassionate. So there can be positive attachment in this sense of active engagement.

Buddhist masters have long used the term "attachment" to describe the quality of compassion for others. For example, a verse from Haribhadra's *Clear Meaning Commentary* refers to compassion that is attached to other living beings.[59] And as we have seen, Nagarjuna teaches that attachment for other living beings will arise spontaneously in the person who realizes emptiness.

Question: Your Holiness, in American culture many people consider it disgraceful or unacceptable to show weakness, pain, or need. How can one show compassion by helping someone if that person is unwilling to admit pain or need by asking for help?

Answer: I don't know. I think it would be better to ask someone with the right sort of expertise.

Question: How is it possible to maintain the practice of nongrasping when grieving the death of someone that you love, especially when it is a sudden death and one is in great shock?

Answer: It is often this way. Much depends on your overall outlook. Seeing the illusionlike nature of reality certainly does have an impact.

I do think it is important to make a distinction between two forms of grasping. When someone generates strong compassion for a suffering being, they have genuine attachment to, focus upon, or engagement with that being. This sort of attachment, engagement, turning towards and holding—it is not a distorted form of grasping. It is not the form of grasping that we need to eliminate.

What we want to eliminate is grasping that is grounded upon falsification of the object, distortions that arise as afflictions grasp at the apparent substantial existence of an object. Some texts say that mental states such as compassion and faith are, by their very nature, virtuous and thus cannot at the same time be afflicted mental states. Yet there are other texts that refer to "afflicted compassion" or "afflicted faith." For those of us who have not realized emptiness, when we generate strong devotion toward the Buddha perhaps there is within that faith, within that devotion, an element of grasping at the Buddha as substantially real. This makes it an instance of so-called "afflicted devotion."

Still, it is important to distinguish grasping rooted in falsification and distortion from the attachment, focus, or holding that we associate with compassion. In our immediate experience, these two forms of grasping may seem the same, but in terms of the overall mental environment they are quite different. Compassion is fact-based, while distorted grasping is not.

It seems that we can have some understanding that things lack independent existence without this directly affecting our afflictions. But gradually our understanding of emptiness changes our whole attitude toward external objects and, especially, internal objects. Gradually, this reduces our afflictions, or at least reduces their intensity, and strengthens our virtuous attitudes. These things can vary according to the physical constitution and mental disposition of the individual.

CHAPTER FOUR

Buddhist Answers to Big Questions

AT AN INTERFAITH meeting in India, I was with a Jew and a Sufi Muslim. We were each posed three questions: What is the self? Does the self have a beginning? Does the self ever end? Different traditions give different answers to these questions.

In answering the first question, we arrive at the real demarcation between Buddhist and non-Buddhist thought. Non-Buddhist Indian traditions—whether theistic or nontheistic—all accept some type of soul theory, some notion of an independent self that owns the body and mind. The Buddha's teaching emphasizes that there is no independent soul or independent self. That is, Buddhism rejects any notion of a self that is independent of the physical and mental elements of the individual. We accept a conventionally existing self that is designated in relation to the mind and body. Of course, when it comes to identifying the exact nature of the self, there is a wide range of positions even within the Buddhist tradition.

Every Event Is Caused

When we turn to the second question, whether there is a beginning, we are dealing with the question of the existence of God. In Christianity, there really is a beginning—God created everything, so this very life is created by God. I think this is a wonderful concept, a great teaching, because the purpose, the very heart, of Christianity is love, affection. So knowing that this very life was created by God brings a powerful feeling of intimacy with God, a sense that God is your own mother. We know that our bodies come from our mothers; they come from our parents, but particularly from our mothers. Even animals feel so close to their mothers. In that same intimate sense, when you feel that this very life is a gift from God, then you are for that reason very, very close to God. And through this sense of intimacy, you become more willing to listen to God's advice. You really want to know what God wants.

In nontheistic religions, including Buddhism, there is no divine Creator; we have instead the law of causality. Things arise in dependence upon causes and conditions. Causes are the creator of the result—and each cause is also the result of previous causes. As far as Buddhism is concerned, it is illogical to conceive of a beginning without a cause. Every event must have its own causes.

When teaching the twelve links of dependent origination, Tsong-kha-pa explains the Buddha's understanding of the origination of things. There he cites the Buddha's teaching of dependent origination wherein the Buddha states (1) because this exists, that exists and (2) because this has arisen, that arises.[60] In the first statement, the Buddha points out that things come into being from their causes and conditions. This notion of conditioning indicates the lack of prior intelligent design. Things do not come into being as a result of some divine intelligence, some earlier intelligence that designs them and brings them forth. Rather each thing comes into being from its own causes.

Then, when the Buddha says, "because this has arisen, that arises," the point is that not only do things originate from their causes, but that causes themselves are impermanent. The causes of things are themselves products of their own corresponding causes. In this way, there is a chain of causation. Events arise from transient causes, causes that in turn have arisen from *their* causes, and so forth.

When you trace back the chain of causation from a Buddhist point of view, you run into problems if you try to posit a beginning. When you posit a beginning, you have to accept that this beginning itself is either caused or uncaused. If you say that the beginning is totally uncaused, then you have a problem. How will you account for the fact that everything begins at one particular point in time rather than another? That is, at some point—and not at another—the whole chain of causation starts up. What is the difference between one circumstance and the other? This seems to force us to accept the presence of some cause, some condition, that makes a difference in the case when there *is* a beginning.

So if you say that there is an absolute beginning, a first event, you will probably have to accept that this beginning does have a cause—a permanent cause, an eternal and unchanging Creator. Here again, from the Buddhist point of view, the problem with a permanent or eternal cause is that you will then have to maintain that this cause either (1) can never produce an effect at all, or (2) should produce the same effect continuously. One cannot say that something is a permanent, eternal, unchanging cause if it sometimes does and sometimes does not give rise to its effect. If you have a cause that sometimes does and sometimes does not give rise to its effect, then clearly it is not permanent. It is not unchanging. It is changing in dependence upon the presence or absence of some other condition.

On these considerations, Buddhism rejects any notion of a beginning to the causal chain. An absolute beginning would have to be either uncaused or caused by a permanent entity—and neither option is logically tenable.

The Buddha taught that because of ignorance, karmic activity arises.[61] As we have seen, things come into being from their causes and conditions—and these causes and conditions are themselves impermanent. But beyond that, it is *not* the case that just any thing produces any other thing, or that each thing produces every other thing. Rather, there is a commensurate relationship between causes and effects so that the specific characteristics of the effects are dependent upon the specific characteristics and qualities of the causes.

In the case of the twelve links of dependent origination, the first cause in the chain is ignorance. At the natural level, no one loves suffering and wishes for it—but just the same, we keep creating the conditions for suffering. So the root cause of our suffering is ignorance. It is the first link in a cycle of conditions.

We Have No Absolute Beginning

Buddhists accept a conventionally existing self, a self that is designated in relation to the combination of body and mind. Therefore, in order to say whether the self has a beginning, we have to decide whether we can posit a beginning for the stream of physical and mental aggregates. This stream or continuum is the actual basis in relation to which the notion of self arises. In terms of a person, the aggregates (*skandhas*) are form—e.g., the body—which has material properties, and four mental aggregates that are not physical and have the nature of subjective experience.

While there is also a very subtle level of form, the word "form" usually refers to the material body of this life. Each person's body changes from lifetime to lifetime. While there are many different kinds of physical objects, if we consider the stream of elementary materials that make up their existence, it is very difficult to posit a real beginning. Our current scientific perspective is that the source for all of the material phenomena in the natural world, including the material of our physical bodies, can be traced back to the very beginning of the universe. It has been suggested that this beginning was a Big Bang.

But even here, we have to ask, Where did the Big Bang come from? What set the stage for that event? There must have been tremendous energy for such an explosion to happen. Is that energy associated with some substance? What causes and conditions brought it about? Therefore, I think it is very difficult to accept an absolute beginning to material existence. Things arise from causes that are earlier moments in a continuum, a stream of change.

We can also consider whether consciousness has a beginning. Since our bodies change from lifetime to lifetime, the more enduring continuum for our individual existence involves the mind, the mental aggregates. When we say that the person or the self is designated in relation to the continuum of the aggregates, we mainly mean that the person is designated on the basis of a stream of subjective experience. The continuum of consciousness has no form. It has no shape and no color. Yet it does have definite effects; our choices clearly lead to experiences of happiness and suffering.

When we seek to understand consciousness, we attribute its existence to the preceding stream of experience with the same characteristics. We can trace the source and continuum of our physical body back to our parents' regenerative fluids, but we cannot likewise trace the source of our consciousness, our mind, back to our parents' consciousnesses. The main cause, the substantial cause, of our consciousness must be a prior moment of consciousness in that very continuum. If we wanted to posit an absolute beginning to our consciousness, we would have two choices. We could say that the very first instance of consciousness came from nowhere as a totally uncaused phenomenon. Or else we could admit that at some point consciousness arose from causes that did not share its same nature and had very different characteristics. Either way, it seems very difficult to posit an absolute beginning to consciousness.

It is not just Buddhists who accept the notion of previous lives, the idea of rebirth; many philosophical traditions subscribe to this idea. One of the key arguments for this view is the empirical evidence of individuals who recall their experience in past lives. I personally met a very young Indian girl whose memory of her past life was extremely convincing. In effect, she had four parents—the two of this life, and also the parents of the immediately previous life. Her parents from the previous life also accepted this young girl as their daughter. Such cases give some clear indication that there are past lives. I was told of another case in which a Tibetan boy was able to read before being taught. And we heard of a case where a young person had very clear memories of a past life, recognized friends, recalled his own name, and even recalled specific items from his house, including books—even though, in that case, he could not actually read. We need further investigation of such cases. Is there some way to understand these situations in terms of genetic disposition? I really don't know. But the answer from the Buddhist point of view is that *there is no beginning* to the continuity of mind.

Is There an End?

The third question is: Is there an end? Within the Buddhist tradition there are two different positions on this. There is one school of thought that maintains that when one attains the final nirvana, the great nirvana, this is a *nirvana without residue.* By that term they mean that the individual—the continuum of the self—completely ceases to exist. It is like the flame of a butter lamp just burning out. However, this is not Tsong-kha-pa's view.

A Buddhist is one who goes to the three jewels for refuge. When the objects of refuge are described in the texts, the Buddha is described as "the supreme among bipeds" (e.g., humans). The Dharma is described as the supreme teaching or the supreme truth. It is a truth that is free from attachment; it is tranquil. It is peace. The Sangha is described as the supreme assembly. However, if we understand the nature and characteristics of the three jewels only at that level, it is not necessarily unique to Buddhism. Other spiritual traditions take refuge and such qualities of the object of refuge may be present in those other traditions. Most—maybe all—spiritual traditions see their own original teacher as supreme among human beings. They will probably say that their spiritual teaching represents a truth that is peaceful and beyond attachment. Likewise, they also have some notion of a spiritual community.

Thus, if you understand the three jewels only on that level, your understanding is not so deep. How can you even say that going for refuge in the three jewels is what defines someone as a practicing Buddhist? People do say this, but how can they explain it? We have to cultivate a deeper understanding of the nature of the Buddha and the nature of Dharma. What is the nature of the Buddha to whom we go for refuge? And what is the particular nature of the Sangha that we as Buddhists perceive to be the supreme community?

With respect to the Buddha, there is a divergence of opinion within the Buddhist tradition. As I mentioned, some maintain that when the Buddha attained final nirvana, the entire continuum of the Buddha's existence came to an end. The other view, which Tsong-kha-pa shares, involves understanding buddhahood in terms of four embodiments.[62] Here, the idea of an absolute end to the continuity of the Buddha's existence is rejected.

Nagarjuna, particularly in his *Sixty Stanzas of Reasoning*, makes a very explicit argument against the idea that the Buddha's final nirvana constituted the absolute end of the Buddha's existence.[63] Nagarjuna says that if that were the case, then the whole concept of someone attaining nirvana without residue would be incoherent. When the person is alive, nirvana without residue is not yet present; yet when the nirvana without residue is reached, the person is no longer there. Thus, the idea of someone's attaining nirvana without residue is incoherent if it involves an absolute end to the continuity of the individual.

The tremendous differences between arhats[64] and buddhas make it untenable that the entirety of the path to buddhahood could be included within the thirty-seven aspects of the path to enlightenment.[65] Buddhas cannot simply be those who have done these same practices for a longer period. The outcomes attained by arhats and by buddhas are so vastly different that, in addition to the thirty-seven aspects, the path to buddhahood must also include other practices such as the six perfections.[66]

We have many mental states that are distorted due to being grounded in a false way of understanding and perceiving the world. These mental states can be stopped, brought to an end, by powerful antidotes to this false way of understanding. However, the essential quality of mind itself is *clear and knowing*. Unlike the case of ignorance or delusion—which can be eliminated—there are no forces or reasons that would block this continuum from going forward. There isn't anything that undermines the continuing existence of the essential quality of the mind itself.

Furthermore, from the highest yoga tantra point of view, when we understand how consciousness operates at a very subtle level, we find two characteristics.[67] One is the *knowing* aspect. And right with it there is a moving, dynamic aspect; we could call it energy. These two aspects are inseparable in that neither can exist without the other. So consciousness continues to exist at this very subtle level right together with this energy.

What happens when a person gains full enlightenment? The consciousness itself, being dependently arisen, is fundamentally empty; emptiness is the ultimate nature of the mind. When one attains buddhahood, this emptiness is the natural body of a buddha, a buddha's body as the very nature of reality. While the ordinary person's mind is pure and unpolluted in its essential nature, it is still tainted by adventitious pollutants and stains. When one attains buddhahood, these adventitious pollutants are removed, so the natural purity of the mind is accompanied by a purity attained through cultivation of the path. Therefore, the emptiness of the mind—the very nature of the person's mind—becomes the natural embodiment of a buddha.

At that point, the person's consciousness becomes a buddha's embodiment of truth as wisdom (*yeshe chögu*) and the energy accompanying that wisdom-mind becomes a buddha's embodiment as form (*zug-gu*). Within the buddha's embodiment as form, there are the speech and physical qualities of a buddha. Buddhahood is thus a state in which body, speech, and mind have become totally inseparable, a single nature, because they are all immediate expressions of the unity of the very subtlest mind and subtlest energy.

The effort to attain buddhahood is fundamentally motivated by an altruistic intention to work for the welfare of an infinite number of living beings for as long as space remains, to the furthest reaches of space. Once buddhahood is attained, that buddha does not cease to exist. The motivation for practice on the bodhisattva path comes to final fruition in an enlightened being who goes on acting for the benefit of all living beings for as long as space remains.

Understanding buddhahood in this manner changes your understanding of the Buddha as an object of refuge. Maitreya's *Sublime Continuum* tells us that a key quality of the Dharma is that it is not just freedom from attachment—it is beyond any concept, beyond anything we can imagine, beyond any verbal expression.[68] The Sangha is a community of practitioners who embody a Dharma that has these inconceivable characteristics. When you have that kind of understanding of the three jewels, it transfigures your understanding of that to which you go for refuge. Implicitly, then, going for refuge to the three jewels becomes an affirmation of the four seals of the Buddha's teaching.[69] Becoming a Buddhist in philosophical terms converges with the act of going for refuge.

CHAPTER FIVE

Four Noble Truths

Instructions for Liberation

TSONG-KHA-PA (I: 34 and 69) refers to the question of how to lead students with "actual instructions." This term refers to the *instructions of the Buddha*. As I have explained, what makes instructions distinctly Buddhist is their relevance to *liberation*. When Tsong-kha-pa presents practices for the person of medium capacity, he (I: 267) explains liberation:

> Liberation means freedom from bondage, and what binds you to cyclic existence is karma and the afflictions. . . . Since this is the nature of bondage, freedom from rebirth impelled by karma and the afflictions is liberation, and the desire to obtain that freedom is the mind intent on liberation.

The notion of liberation is common in the classical traditions of India. In the Buddhist context, liberation is generally defined as a mental state—or else a quality of mind—that involves freedom from some contamination or stain. Of course, for Buddhists the notion of liberation is tied intimately to the view of selflessness. Nagarjuna gives a precise explanation in his *Fundamental Wisdom of the Middle Way*, where he says that one gains freedom by stopping karma and afflictions, karma and afflictions arise from false conceptualizations, and these conceptualizations can be calmed by emptiness.[70] On this reading, Nagarjuna explains emptiness as a *means* for stopping afflictions and karma.

An alternative reading of the Sanskrit text says that false conceptualizations are calmed not *by* emptiness but *within* emptiness. Cyclic existence (*samsara*) arises on the basis of our distorted understanding of the fundamental nature of mind. So insight into the nature of mind brings about the calming and dissolution of all stains and distortions within the nature of the mind itself. Nagarjuna takes liberation to be the very nature of a mind at the point when all false conceptualizations have been dissolved.

Tsong-kha-pa identifies karma and the afflictions as what bind us; he identifies cyclic existence as the condition in which we are bound. Cyclic existence means conditioned existence with mental and physical aggregates that one has appropriated, taken up under the influence of afflictions and karma. So cyclic existence does not mean having just any kind of mind and body; there *can* be existence with uncontaminated aggregates, liberated existence. Cyclic existence means being born with *karmically conditioned* aggregates. It is cyclic because we continue to exist in this way, going from one set of aggregates to another. Karma and the afflictions trap us here, so there is an element of constraint, a lack of freedom on our part. Dharmakirti's *Commentary on the Compendium of Valid Cognition* identifies the karmically conditioned aggregates themselves as the cyclic existence within which we suffer.[71]

The Order of the Four Noble Truths

In discussing the Buddha's teaching of true suffering as the first noble truth, Tsong-kha-pa (1: 269) first raises a qualm: "True origins are the causes and true sufferings are their effects. Why then did the Blessed One reverse that order?" In fact, the origin of suffering must precede suffering. Maitreya's *Ornament of Clear Realization* explains suffering and its origin in this actual sequence, with origins first and then sufferings that arise as a result, etc.[72] However, Tsong-kha-pa (1: 269) explains that, when the Buddha first gave the sermon on the four noble truths, "the Teacher reversed the sequence of cause and effect" for a specific purpose. It is only when one comes to understand the nature of suffering that true aspiration to seek freedom from that suffering really arises. Therefore, the Buddha teaches the truth of suffering first. The Buddha insists that we must first recognize suffering *as* suffering.

Of course, when we talk about suffering in the context of the four noble truths, we are not talking about suffering in the usual sense. Ordinarily, we take pleasurable experiences and mundane successes as desirable; we do not see them as being in the nature of suffering. When we speak of happiness, we usually mean something that is wonderful or successful in a worldly way. Examining our own attitudes toward people who are successful in worldly terms, we find that we feel admiration and sometimes even envy. Actually, what they have is what we wish to have. So instead of recognizing worldly success to be in the nature of suffering, we take it to be happiness. We need to cultivate a deeper understanding of true sufferings.

The Panchen Lama Losang Chogyen[73] sums it up quite beautifully. He says that there are many ways in which one can contemplate the nature of suffering. At the first level, evident suffering is something even animals recognize as undesirable and try to escape. At the second level, the suffering of change is something toward which non-Buddhist practitioners cultivate a sense of disenchantment as they seek to attain the pleasures of elevated meditative states of concentration and formless absorption.[74] But when the Buddha talks about cultivating a true recognition of the meaning of suffering, he means that we need to understand the third level of suffering, the suffering of conditioning. Our very existence is driven and conditioned by karma and afflictions. Tsong-kha-pa and the Panchen Lama point out that our aggregates serve both as conditions for the arising of future suffering and as containers within which we are presently bound in suffering as our past karma ripens. If you can recognize suffering in this sense, then you will be able to generate a genuine aspiration to get out of this sort of conditioned existence. This is renunciation.

Tsong-kha-pa (1: 269) writes:

> Once you recognize suffering, you see yourself as submerged in an ocean of suffering, and you realize that, if you want to be liberated from suffering, you must counteract it. Moreover, you recognize that you cannot stop suffering unless you counteract its cause. By investigating the cause of suffering, you come to understand its true origin. Consequently, the Buddha spoke next about the truth of origin.

And he continues:

> Next you develop an understanding of the truth of the origin, an understanding that contaminated karma produces the suffering of cyclic existence, that afflictions produce karma, and that the conception of self is the root of the afflictions. When you see that you can eliminate the conception of self, you will vow to realize its cessation, which is also the cessation of suffering.

Later Tsong-kha-pa explains this conception of self more specifically, relating it to the teachings on emptiness. But here he is presenting the general consensus among all the Buddhist schools that grasping at self is the root of cyclic existence. Suffering arises from its origin, its origin is constituted principally by karma and the afflictions, and the root of all the afflictions is the grasping at self.

Changing Our Minds

In cyclic existence, we all have a sense of grasping at self. It is an innate mental state, not something acquired intellectually through philosophical training. It is a very natural state of mind. But is it *correct*? Does it accord with the reality? Just because a perception or a mental state is natural does not mean that it accords with how things are. We must ask this question and probe into this. And when we do, we come to recognize that grasping at self is really a form of ignorance. It is a distortion.

Things appear to us in one way, but they actually exist in a different way. When we react to events with afflictive emotion, we just react and operate on the level of ordinary appearances. Things appear to us as possessing some kind of independent reality of their own and we tend to affirm that perception immediately, accepting as real that apparent separateness and solidity. We react on the basis of our acceptance of that perception. We then grasp very strongly at the apparent solidity of the objects we perceive. Thus, we are not reacting to things as they actually are.

We have to investigate the disparity between reality and our perceptions. We can learn to differentiate our accustomed perception of reality from reality itself. To do this, we have to have some way of understanding the true mode of being, the actual way that things exist. In Buddhist texts all of the reasoning about emptiness comes down to just this: the importance of establishing proper understanding of the actual nature of reality. When we understand emptiness, then we see that our naïve perception of things as having self-existence is distorted. And because this perception is distorted, all of the afflictions based upon it are unstable. They can be rooted out and cleared from our mental states.

We also need to recognize that the essential nature of the mind is not polluted. A person may be temperamentally inclined to hatefulness, but even so he will not *always* be full of hate. He may experience moments of loving-kindness, moments of compassion. Loving-kindness and hatred are diametrically opposed mental states; they cannot coexist in a single individual in a single moment. That even the hateful person is not openly hateful all the time and has occasional moments of compassion shows that the essential nature of the mind is not inseparable from afflictions such as hatred. The essential nature of the mind is such as to allow the arising of afflictions as well as mental states that oppose these afflictions.

Likewise, our grasping at the self-existence of things may seem well established, normal and natural, but that does not mean that it is integral to the mind's nature. By cultivating the wisdom of selflessness we can gradually undermine this grasping. Eventually we can recognize the utter absence of self-existence. This illustrates that no matter how strong a particular affliction may be, it is not an integral, inseparable element of the mind.

These two points are very important: (1) The afflictions—particularly ignorance that is their root—are distorted and thus unstable; and (2) the afflictions can be separated from the essential nature of the mind. These points allow you to know that our innate sense of grasping at self-existence is a removable mental state. Then, when you hear about the cessation of suffering, you will have a sincere feeling with a distinctive flavor. You will aspire to that freedom and set out to attain it. Tsong-kha-pa (1: 270) says, "In this way, when you do think, 'I shall realize the cessation that is liberation,' you become interested in the truth of the path."

Understanding Dependent Arising

Your notion of what constitutes the fundamental ignorance at the root of cyclic existence depends upon your view of reality. In the case of Nagarjuna, his final position appears in the *Seventy Stanzas on Emptiness*, where he writes that while phenomena arise from causes and conditions, ignorance grasps at phenomena as possessing final existence.[75] Ignorance is a mental state that conceives of dependently originated phenomena as having a final reality of their own. To make this clearer, Aryadeva's *Four Hundred* teaches that just as the sense of touch pervades the body, including the other sense faculties, delusion (ignorance) permeates all of the afflictions. Aryadeva then explains ignorance or delusion by way of its antidote, stating that ignorance will no longer arise in the person who sees dependent origination.[76] Therefore, we should really delve into and get to the bottom of the teachings on dependent origination.

Nagarjuna's *Seventy Stanzas on Emptiness* cites the fact that phenomena come into being in dependence upon causes and conditions as the proof that they lack ultimate existence.[77] Emptiness is thus established by taking the fact of causal origination as the premise. Generally speaking, we are naturally aware of causal relationships. To some extent, at a very gross level, even animals are capable of making causal connections. They know that if they eat, they won't be hungry; if they're feeling too hot, they will look for shade. In considering our own future welfare, humans are more capable than animals. We try to save for the future. We try to better educate ourselves so that we will qualify for jobs with bigger paychecks, perhaps with a better-known company. We make causal connections between what we want in the future and the conditions that are necessary to get there. We organize our efforts on the basis of our understanding of such connections.

Nagarjuna helps us to reflect more deeply upon the implications of these cause-and-effect relationships. How is it that effects depend on causes? It is by way of the interdependent nature of reality. Cause-and-effect relationships operate because cause and effect are not separate, enclosed realities. There is an openness in things that allows for relationships to occur. Because relationships are possible, events can relate to each other as cause and effect.

Nagarjuna shows us that by reflecting deeply upon cause and effect we can come to recognize the interrelatedness of things. When you recognize things as having a relational, dependent nature, then you come to see that all phenomena are devoid of their own self-enclosed, intrinsic reality. You then can understand how things exist in terms of designation and convention. Therefore, when the Buddha taught dependent origination in terms of causes and effects in the twelve links, he did not explicitly teach emptiness, but he provided the foundation that allows us to understand emptiness.[78]

We can consider the Buddha's teaching on dependent origination both (1) at the level of cause and effect and (2) in terms of emptiness. The first pertains to developing the conditions for attainment of favorable rebirth in higher realms of existence. The second pertains to the cultivation of the causes and conditions for the attainment of liberation. So dependent origination is vital both to our immediate aim (favorable rebirth) and our long-term aim (liberation). I think that this is why Tsong-kha-pa says that dependent arising is the most precious jewel in the treasury of the Buddha's teachings.[79]

When we set out to realize these two aims, favorable rebirth has to come first; only on that basis can we realize the second aim, liberation. This is because the practice of the path leading to liberation requires the maximum use of our faculty of intelligence. Human existence has the most advanced form of intelligence. This is why Nagarjuna's *Precious Garland* first presents all the practices aimed at obtaining fortunate rebirth and then goes on to other teachings. Similarly, Aryadeva's *Four Hundred* presents a three-stage sequence of practices: first, you must stop nonvirtuous activity; then, you must cease grasping at self; and finally, you must cease grasping at all false views.[80] Again, in the stages of the path literature, you begin with preoccupations totally confined to this life, progress to concerns with one's next life, and then eventually develop a motivation to attain liberation.

Tsong-kha-pa (1: 270) writes:

> [T]he four truths are taught repeatedly throughout the Mahayana and the lesser vehicle teachings. Since the Sugata[81] has included in the four truths the vital points concerning the process of cyclic existence and its cessation, this teaching is crucial for achieving freedom. Since this synoptic outline of the practice is important, it must be taught to students in just this order.

Tsong-kha-pa makes a very important point: one must guide students on the basis of the sequence of the four noble truths, these being the actual instructions of the Buddha.

True Sufferings

Tsong-kha-pa 's *Songs of Spiritual Experience* says that if you do not work at contemplating the faults of true sufferings, then you will not develop an authentic aspiration to liberation.[82] If you believe that existence in cyclic existence is not such a big problem—or that it is actually quite joyful—then you simply will have no real wish for freedom from it.

At the same time, if you do not contemplate the conditions that drive cyclic existence—the origins of suffering—then you will not know how to sever the roots of misery. Even if you recognize the suffering nature of cyclic existence, simply making a wish or prayer to be free from it is not going to help you escape. You have to think about what conditions lead to that suffering. So Tsong-kha-pa teaches that we need to cultivate both disenchantment about cyclic existence and recognition of the factors that bind us within it.

In the *Great Treatise* Tsong-kha-pa (1: 265-295) presents contemplation of the nature of suffering in three broad sections: (1) contemplation of the eight types of suffering; (2) contemplation of the six types of suffering; and (3) further meditations on suffering. About the eighth of the eight types of suffering, Tsong-kha-pa (1: 279) says:

> The Buddha said, "In brief, the five appropriated aggregates are suffering." Reflection on the meaning of this teaching again takes in five points. It is the nature of the five aggregates appropriated by karma and the afflictions to be:
> (1) vessels for future suffering;
> (2) vessels for suffering based on what presently exists;
> (3) vessels for the suffering of pain;
> (4) vessels for the suffering of change; and
> (5) vessels for the suffering of conditionality.
> Reflect on these again and again.
>
> Here, with regard to the first point, you induce suffering in future lives by taking up these appropriated aggregates.

Our mental and physical aggregates arise through the conditioning of karma and afflictions, so they have a character and nature that is very close to that of karma and afflictions. They have a quality of being vulnerable to further aggravation by karma and afflictions, so they are receptive to suffering. In this sense, they are "vessels for future suffering."

During the time of the Twelfth Dalai Lama, there was a very learned Mongolian scholar who happened to be involved in something that led to his being reprimanded. He was slightly disgraced and was feeling really sorry for himself. He then touched his own body and said, "Well, all of this pain and all of this misery becomes possible because I happened to have this karmically conditioned, appropriated body." The Buddhist point of view is that all problems in the world, both societal and individual, happen because our existence is conditioned by karma and by afflictions. They are what give us the kind of mind and body that is the basis for all these sufferings to arise.

Tsong-kha-pa (1: 279) writes:

> As for the second point, the appropriated aggregates form the basis for states, such as illness and old age, that are grounded in the already existing aggregates. The third and the fourth points both come about because the appropriated aggregates are linked with dysfunctional tendencies toward these two types of suffering.

"These two types of suffering" refers to evident suffering and the suffering of change. Tsong-kha-pa (1: 279) continues:

> As regards the fifth point, the very existence of the appropriated aggregates constitutes the nature of the suffering of conditionality because all of the compositional factors which depend on previous karma and afflictions are the suffering of conditionality.

Passing over Tsong-kha-pa's (1: 281-287) discussion of the six types of suffering, we come to the three types of suffering. Of the second of these, the suffering of change, Tsong-kha-pa (1: 289) writes:

> Pleasant feelings experienced by beings in cyclic existence are like the pleasure felt when cool water is applied to an inflamed boil or carbuncle: as the temporary feeling fades, the pain reasserts itself.

This is one reason why even what we conventionally identify as pleasurable experiences are recognized to be ultimately in the nature of suffering. Dharmakirti's *Commentary on the Compendium of Valid Cognition* points out that impermanence must lead us to recognize the suffering nature of our existence.[83] The very same causes and conditions that give rise to things simultaneously equip them with a transient nature, a quality of being not only subject to change, but actually changing instant by instant.

One Buddhist school, the Vaibhashika, presents impermanence in terms of an end to the continued existence of a thing. They speak of what is known as the four characteristics of conditioned phenomena: arising, enduring, decay, and then cessation. But all other Buddhist schools understand impermanence in terms of moment by moment existence, the momentary quality of things. The fact that a phenomenon is momentary is not contingent upon its contact with some new condition. Rather, the very cause that creates a phenomenon brings it into being as something with a transitory nature.

The natures of transient phenomena are governed by their causes and conditions. So in the particular case of our current situation, what are the causes and conditions governing us? They are karma and the afflictions. In terms of the teaching on the twelve links of dependent origination, the first in the chain is fundamental ignorance. Even the term ignorance (*ma rig pa*) suggests something negative.[84] With such a negative cause, the result is bound to be negative as well. Reflecting on this carefully, we find that there is really no basis for any sense of satisfaction in cyclic existence.

Carrying on the same metaphor that he used earlier, Tsong-kha-pa (1: 290) explains the suffering of conditionality:

> Contaminated neutral feelings are like an inflamed boil which is in contact with neither soothing nor irritating substances. Because these feelings coexist with dysfunctional tendencies, they constitute *the suffering of conditionality*, which, as explained above, does not refer to the feelings alone.

Tsong-kha-pa earlier explained that it is not only our feelings, but all of the mental states and mental factors concomitant with them, that belong to the category of suffering. He (1: 289) writes:

> This is called *the suffering of change* and includes not only the feeling itself, but also the main mind and other mental processes that are similar to it, as well as the contaminated objects which, when perceived, give rise to that feeling.

Pleasurable, painful, and neutral feelings are suffering, all are unsatisfactory. All of the mental states associated with those feelings are suffering; the sensory faculties and their objects, which give rise to those feelings, are suffering. They all engender suffering, so they are classified together.

The Four Seals of the Dharma

Among the four seals of the Buddha's teaching,[85] the first is that *all conditioned phenomena are impermanent* or transient; the second is that *all contaminated phenomena are in the nature of suffering*. This is Tsong-kha-pa's point. Yet after explaining that all conditioned phenomena are impermanent and that all contaminated phenomena are in the nature of suffering, the Buddha does not stop. Perhaps saying *only* this would cause further depression and a sense of discouragement. Is this suffering endless? Or is there a way to stop it?

This is why the third seal is very important. The Buddha teaches that *all phenomena are empty and devoid of self*. Of course there are different ways to explain the teaching of selflessness in different schools of Buddhist philosophy. Still, in general, all Buddhist schools accept that it is grasping at self-existence that lies at the root of our suffering. This is the root of all other afflictions. In fact, this grasping at self-existence can be demonstrated to be a distorted way to perceive and experience the world. It is not consonant with reality. Hence, there is a powerful antidote to it and we can cultivate that antidote. This powerful antidote, when applied, can eliminate and eradicate grasping at self. Therefore, the Buddha teaches the fourth seal: *nirvana is true peace.* By applying a powerful antidote against the root of suffering, which is grasping at self, we can develop insight into the nature of reality. This will lead to the attainment of nirvana, true peace. It is beautiful to connect the four seals with the four noble truths, taking them to heart in an integrated way.

Tsong-kha-pa (1: 290) says:

> Insofar as the suffering of conditionality is affected by previous karma, as well as the afflictions, and coexists with seeds that will produce future suffering and affliction, it coexists with persistent dysfunctional tendencies.

He then explains why the suffering of conditionality is so pervasive, citing (1: 291) the *Descent into the Womb Sutra*:

> Nanda, the physical activities of walking, sitting, standing, or lying down must each be understood as suffering. If meditators analyze the nature of these physical activities, they will see that if they spend the day walking and do not rest, sit down, or lie down, they will experience walking exclusively as suffering and will experience intense, sharp, unbearable and unpleasant feelings. The notion that walking is pleasant will not arise.

Nanda was the Buddha's brother. Tsong-kha-pa (1: 291) further cites that same sutra:

> Nanda, when this contaminated feeling of pleasure arises, it is only suffering that is arising; when it ends, it is only this nature of suffering that ends. When it arises yet again, it is only a conditioned phenomenon that arises; when it ends, it is only a conditioned phenomenon that ends.

This point is that the suffering of conditioning pervades every aspect of our existence. If we want to follow the Buddha's advice that we must recognize the truth of suffering, then we have to contemplate these explanations.

Where Does Suffering Come From?

We also must abandon the origin of suffering. In explaining the nature of the afflictions, Tsong-kha-pa (1: 298) cites Asanga's *Compendium of Knowledge*:

> An affliction is defined as a phenomenon that, when it arises, is disturbing in character and that, through arising, disturbs the mind-stream.[86]

The mind has a natural state of equilibrium. Certain mental states, thoughts, or emotions tend to disturb that equilibrium. Afflictions have this quality. This effect can range from very gross to very subtle.

Among Buddhist schools of thought, there are those that accept the notion of inherent existence and there is the Prasangika Madhyamaka school which totally rejects inherent existence. The first group of Buddhist schools has a broad consensus on the nature of afflictions. However, the Prasangika Madhyamaka has a much subtler way of understanding what constitutes grasping at true existence. The idea of a very subtle form of grasping at true existence changes the way they understand afflictions such as attachment, aversion, delusion, and so on.

Asanga's definition of affliction can perhaps be accepted if we read it in a very broad sense. What does he mean by "disturbance" or "disequilibrium"? We could make a number of guesses; I will suggest one idea. Note that Tsong-kha-pa (1: 300) concludes his explanation of how afflictions arise with these words:

> I have explained these ten afflictions in accordance with Asanga's *Compendium of Knowledge* and *Levels of Yogic Deeds* and with Vasubandhu's *Explanation of the Five Aggregates.*[87]

We may read this as implying that Tsong-kha-pa thinks there is a different and subtler way to understand the afflictions. Perhaps we need to add a qualification: causing this disturbance *without any control on our part.* When a practitioner cultivates compassion, the experience becomes quite strong as you feel someone else's pain; there really is an element of disturbance. Yet that kind of disturbance does not arise without any control on one's part. There is a voluntary dimension to this because you are choosing to share in others' suffering, intentionally cultivating that compassion. Disturbing emotions that seem to arise spontaneously tend to be negative. Emotions arising from intentional training in which we reflect and reason—these are usually positive.

CHAPTER SIX

How to Practice

TSONG-KHA-PA EXPLAINS how students should rely on a spiritual teacher and how the teacher should lead students in the actual instructions of the Buddha. All of the Buddha's teachings are aimed at bringing about the realization of our immediate aim—rebirth into a high realm—and our long-term aim—attaining liberation. In order to guide students in these instructions, the spiritual teacher needs to have certain qualities. The effectiveness of teaching always depends on the quality of the teacher. For example, when we choose a university or a school, we know that the quality of the school is mainly determined by the quality of the professors or the teachers working there.

The Buddha outlined in various texts the qualities that teachers need for specific types of instruction, from monastic discipline to highest yoga tantra. For stages of the path teachings, the teacher must be someone who can impart instructions encompassing the practices of persons of all three levels of capacity.[88] Key qualities include the ten listed in Maitreya's *Ornament for the Mahayana Sutras*. Tsong-kha-pa (1: 71) cites a passage from Maitreya's *Ornament for the Mahayana Sutras*:

> Rely on a Mahayana teacher who is disciplined, serene, thoroughly pacified, has good qualities surpassing those of the students, is energetic, has a wealth of scriptural knowledge, possesses loving concern, has thorough knowledge of reality and skill in instructing disciples, and has abandoned dispiritedness.

Tsong-kha-pa (1: 71) explains:

> It is said that those who have not disciplined themselves have no basis for disciplining others. Therefore, gurus who intend to discipline others' minds must first have disciplined their own. How should they have been disciplined? It is not helpful for them to have done just any practice, and then call the outcome a good quality of knowledge. They need a way to discipline the mind that accords with the general teachings of the Conqueror [i.e., the Buddha]. The three precious trainings are definitely such a way.

The Buddha's instructions primarily pertain to the attainment of liberation; the main practices that constitute the path to liberation are the practices of the three higher trainings in ethics, meditative stabilization, and wisdom. Thus, the master who gives these instructions must have disciplined his or her own mind in these trainings and must embody knowledge arising from these trainings. Moreover, since the stages of the path teachings are instructions not only for the attainment of liberation but also for the attainment of the full enlightenment of buddhahood, the teacher must be able to present a path that includes practices such as the spirit of enlightenment and great compassion. And in order to do that properly, the teacher must actually have these qualities.

Maitreya's text adds that the teacher must have a thorough knowledge of reality, which means knowing the ultimate nature of things. This reflects the philosophical view of the author, who presents the Chittamatra school's distinction between the selflessness of persons on the one hand and ultimate reality on the other. Maitreya's text takes wisdom in the context of the three higher trainings as the wisdom of personal selflessness—but *not* as wisdom knowing the ultimate reality. Thus, he lists as an additional quality the realization of ultimate reality—knowledge of the selflessness of *phenomena*—this being the ultimate reality as understood in the Chittamatra system.

Tsong-kha-pa (1: 75) identifies the three main qualities needed in a student of the stages of the path teachings: *impartiality*, *intelligence*, and *diligence*. When searching to understand the nature of reality, it is very important to have an objective or nonpartisan standpoint. Otherwise, you will be swayed by your partiality to one system or one way of explaining things. Such partisanship interferes with understanding the actual nature of reality.

Intelligence here refers to critical intelligence that can discern the difference between what is right and what is wrong, what is correct and what is incorrect. It is a critical, inquiring mental faculty. At the beginning of the practice, you need to have a measure of skepticism, a kind of a doubt. It is extremely important. This is because only this kind of questioning creates a real possibility for deeper understanding. If you approach every teaching right from the beginning with a single-pointed faith, then this possibility does not open up.

The classical Indian tradition identifies the subject matter of each text, the immediate reason for seeking understanding of that subject matter, and the long-term purpose of gaining such knowledge. When a text is written for persons with critical faculties, it is anticipated that such a person will want to know about these factors. Sometimes classical texts anticipate that different people will engage with the text in different ways. Those of slightly inferior faculties may approach scripture with moral faith and devotion, while those with more critical mental faculties will want to know from what point of view the text presents the nature of reality.

Tsong-kha-pa then presents the actual process by which one relies upon the spiritual teacher. What state of mind and what behavior should one adopt? As he explains this, Tsong-kha-pa (1: 86) raises a question:

> We must practice in accordance with the gurus' words. Then what if we rely on the gurus and they lead us to an incorrect path or employ us in activities that are contrary to the three vows? Should we do what they say?

He answers his own question:

> With respect to this, Gunaprabha's *Sutra on the Discipline* states, "If the abbot instructs you to do what is not in accord with the teachings, refuse." Also, the *Cloud of Jewels Sutra* states, "With respect to virtue act in accordance with the gurus' words, but do not act in accord with the gurus' words with respect to nonvirtue." Therefore, you must not listen to nonvirtuous instructions. The twelfth birth story clearly gives us the meaning of not engaging in what is improper.

The twelfth birth story refers to the *Jataka Tales.*[89]

For example, among all of Atisha's teachers, his most important was Serlingpa. Atisha particularly revered Serlingpa for his teachings on the spirit of enlightenment. However, Serlingpa's philosophical standpoint was that of the Chittamatra. Just because Serlingpa was Atisha's most important guru does not mean that Atisha would follow his guru's instructions in every field. He was a devout student of Serlingpa, but in the case of philosophical understanding he followed the Madhyamaka rather than adopting his teacher's Chittamatra standpoint.

Meditation

As he explains how to rely on a spiritual teacher, Tsong-kha-pa (1: 94-99) lays out what to do during a session of formal meditation practice, presenting the six preparatory practices and the seven branches of worship.[90] He then explains (1: 100-108) how to behave in between periods of meditation. It is important to have a balanced diet and to use even sleep as a time to strengthen your practice. You should guard the gates of your senses and live with mindfulness, with care. The point is that the actual formal sitting sessions and the periods in between sessions should be complementary, each enhancing the quality of the other. Learn to use twenty-four hours every day to foster virtue through one means or another.

Nobody wakes up early in the morning thinking, "Today I really should have more trouble. I ought to have more conflicts and anger."

Instead we think, "Today I hope for a very peaceful day, a free and happy day." Nonetheless, we see many problems. On this planet with six billion human beings, no one *wants* trouble. But there is still plenty of trouble—most of it caused by us, by human beings. This seems very clear. We really do want what is good, but our minds are completely dominated by afflictions. These mental afflictions are based upon ignorance at many levels, including the ultimate ignorance and coarser levels of ignorance. These ignorant, deluded minds simply do not know reality. Deluded minds look at things from just one angle and decide, "Oh, this is bad," or "This is good."

Meditation means learning to control our minds, thereby protecting our minds from domination by delusion and other afflictions. We may think, "Oh, I wish my mind were not dominated by ignorance and other afflictions." But these afflictions are very powerful and very destructive; they operate despite our wishes. We have to work to develop effective countermeasures. We cannot buy such remedies from a store; even very sophisticated machines cannot produce them for us. They are obtained only through mental effort, training the mind in meditation. Meditation means making our minds familiar with these countervailing forces, becoming habituated to them day by day, week by week, month by month, year by year. Even lifetime after lifetime, the effort still continues. Gradually, these countervailing forces become stronger and, as they do, the afflictions automatically recede because they are incompatible with these new mental states. The two are contradictory in the sense that they cannot exist together.

The Tibetan equivalent of the term "meditation" is *gomba* (*sgom pa*). It is *bhavana* in Sanskrit, which suggests deliberate cultivation and familiarization. Generally the Tibetan verb *'gom pa* means "habituation" or "becoming familiar," but as *sgom pa* it is an active verb, indicating an agent who deliberately carries out a particular type of familiarization.

The course of our actions is dictated by our minds and our minds in turn are dominated by and dictated to by afflictions. On this account, even though we wish for happiness, we end up with suffering. We are very familiar with and habituated to undisciplined mental states.

Engrained over many lifetimes, such mental states seem spontaneous and natural. When we meditate so as to develop antidotes, we are going against the grain. We are learning new skills, a new way of thinking, a new way of being. So at first these antidotes are very weak, but over time they become stronger and, as they do, the afflictions become weaker.

Afflictions are tremendously diverse and incredibly opportunistic. Whenever there is an opening, they find one way or another to manifest. So it is important to understand them and to recognize them, to know how they appear in our minds. For example, we tend to regard attachment as a friend. It is a quality of our mind that tends to pull others towards us, so it helps us bring together conditions that we deem helpful for our survival. Anger and hatred are mental states that arise in relation to an obstacle; we tend to feel that they are there to protect us against things we don't want. We regard them as trusted friends, safeguarding us.

Responding to the diversity and ingenuity of the afflictions, we need powerful and diverse antidotes. The Buddha taught eighty-four thousand heaps of teachings; the literature explaining these teachings includes huge numbers of extensive treatises. There is a single, ultimate aim behind all of these teachings—to help us to find peace of mind. But we need a vast array of teachings and practices because the afflictions that disturb us are so diverse. Also, they manifest differently in different individuals. If we examine the afflictions themselves, how they function in our minds, and the internal and external conditions that give rise to them, then we are better prepared to develop antidotes. It is not enough to recognize the destructiveness of the afflictions and then make a wish for them to go away. We have to be very deliberate in cultivating their antidotes.

We develop antidotes to the afflictions through a series of levels: (1) wisdom derived from study, (2) wisdom derived from reflection, and (3) wisdom derived from meditation. Wisdom derived from study comes from listening to a teacher or studying a text. In these ways you can develop an intellectual understanding of the characteristics of the afflictions and the appropriate antidotes for each. On the basis of this intellectual understanding, you must then reflect critically and repeatedly, deepening your understanding until you have a genuine sense of conviction about the efficacy of the antidotes.

Up through this second level, your meditation is primarily *analytic*. As you engage in critical reflection and meditative analysis, you have to use reasoning based on four principles, these being the four avenues by which we engage with reality.[91] These are (a) the principle of nature, (b) the principle of dependence, (c) the principle of function, and—on the basis of these first three principles—(d) the principle of evidence. For example, investigating the mind in terms of the principle of nature, we find that it is characterized by being clear and knowing. Again, in terms of the principle of nature, we find that all mental states change moment by moment. They are transient, evanescent. Also within the mind, we see the operation of incompatible contradictories. For example, we know that hatred and anger towards someone are contradictory to loving-kindness and compassion towards that person. These opposing forces contradict one another so that we cannot have both feelings at the same time. They are like heat and cold, opposing each other so as to preclude coexistence. This idea of incompatible contradictories is again part of the principle of nature.

When, based on analysis of nature, you then analyze cause-and-effect relationships, this is the principle of dependence. Recognizing these causal relations, you can come to understand the specific functions of different mental states. That each thing—in this case, each mental state—has its own distinctive function is the principle of function. Then, understanding these three principles, you can use logical evidence. Given that such and such is the case, something else must logically follow.

Using these four principles in analysis, you can bring to bear the correct antidotes against each affliction as it arises in your mind. Based on this sort of analytic meditation, you can then move to the third level—wisdom derived from meditation. Here your meditation becomes more in the nature of absorption, with less analysis. The primary approach is to maintain a single-pointed placement of the mind upon a fact that you have determined in analysis. Through meditating on this fact with single-pointed attention, this fact becomes ever more evident, until you have attained wisdom deriving from meditative practice. These are the steps through which we transform our minds.

Questions for the Dalai Lama

Question: Your Holiness, you have said that we relate to events based on our perceptions, rather than based on reality. We need to differentiate our perceptions from reality. But how will we know reality without being influenced by our perceptions?

Answer: Generally, if you look at a single thing or event from only one angle, then you cannot see the full picture. In order to understand an event you have to look from various different angles. Even in the case of a physical thing, knowing only one of its dimension does not give you the full picture. With three or four or six dimensions, then you can get a clearer picture. It is this way with all things; you have to examine them from various points of view, along various dimensions. Seeing just one aspect, there is always a gap between appearance and reality. This is why investigation is critical. Only through investigation can we reduce the gap between appearance and reality. It is the only way.

Earlier I used the words "reality" and "appearance" within the context of the two truths. How can we get at the root of our suffering? What is the root of our mental afflictions? That root is our grasping at the true existence of things. This deluded mind grasps at true existence, engaging the events of the world primarily in terms of how they appear, at the level of perception. Things appear a certain way and then the mind grasps them as though that appearance were the actual reality of the thing. When you recognize that appearances do not accord with the way things really are, then you can gradually weaken the grip of that grasping.

Question: Your Holiness, as a beginner on the path, still taking just baby steps, do you have any words to help me establish a meaningful daily practice that will lead me forward to greater awareness and understanding?

Answer: Read more. There are translations of Buddhist texts into English, as well as French, German, Spanish, and of course Chinese—although, I think there are fewer translations into Chinese than into English. There are many new translations into English. Read such texts daily for an hour or at least a half hour. Then turn your mind inward and contemplate what you have learned. Examine and investigate, comparing what the text says with your usual way of thinking and living. It is best to do this in the morning, when your mind is fresh. Maybe after breakfast is even better; at least for me it is like that. Before breakfast, I am hungry. Sometimes when I meditate, half of my mind goes to my stomach!

Take this approach. Study, and then take what you have understood as the basis for your contemplation, spending some time each morning in formal meditation. Combine understanding of what you have studied with meditative practice. This approach brings together learning, critical reflection, and meditation.

CHAPTER SEVEN

The Meaning of Human Life

OUR DISCUSSION of meditation shows that analysis is crucial to the process of mental transformation. The wisdom of study and the wisdom of reflection emerge from practice that depends on the proper use of intelligence. Since humans are equipped with the best sort of intelligence, for a Dharma practitioner having a human existence is extremely important.

Having established a relationship with a spiritual teacher, how should we practice? Laying out the stages through which one trains one's mind, Tsong-kha-pa (1: 117-175) begins with a consideration of motivation. A crucial point he makes is the importance of recognizing the preciousness of being born as a human, in particular as a human who has the leisure and opportunity to practice the Dharma. This rare type of rebirth must be used for a great purpose. We cannot take it for granted or assume that we will readily find another human rebirth in the future. So the question is: How can we make our precious human existence meaningful?

To explain this, Tsong-kha-pa (1: 129-141) uses the concept that persons are of three capacities: small, medium, and great. To define the person of small capacity, he (1: 130) cites Atisha's *Lamp for the Path to Enlightenment*:

> Know as the lowest those persons who diligently strive to attain solely the joys of cyclic existence, by any means, for their own welfare alone.

Their primary aim is worldly happiness; their approach to everything is shaped by that motivation.

Atisha's text (cited 1: 130-131) then defines the person of medium capacity:

> Those persons are called "medium" who stop sinful actions, turn their backs on the joys of cyclic existence, and diligently strive just for their own peace.

The main motivation of these individuals is to obtain freedom from cyclic existence; they are deeply disenchanted with all the apparent delights of cyclic existence. Here, "sinful" refers to the afflictions; "sinful actions" means activities that lead to birth in cyclic existence. Practitioners of medium capacity turn away from such actions and diligently strive for their own peace and freedom, liberation from cyclic existence. Their main practices are the three higher trainings in ethics, meditation, and wisdom. In the context of the training in wisdom, they focus on the thirty-seven aspects of the path to enlightenment.

Then Tsong-kha-pa (1: 131) cites Atisha's definition of persons of great capacity:

> Those persons are called "superior" who sincerely want to extinguish all the sufferings of others by understanding their own suffering.

These practitioners have insight into their own suffering and then extend that same understanding to all other beings. They are motivated to end the suffering of all beings and it is on that basis that they aspire to attain buddhahood for the benefit of all beings. They practice both the ultimate and conventional forms of the spirit of enlightenment, as well as the six perfections.[92] These practices are unique to the practitioner of great capacity.

Because of their different aims, there are different practices that are particularly pertinent for each of the three persons. For the practitioner of small capacity, the aim is to attain fortunate rebirth. The person of medium capacity takes up practices intended to bring about liberation from cyclic existence. The person of great capacity wants practices and teachings that will lead to attainment of a buddha's omniscient state.

If we ask what is distinctively Buddhist, what is the nature of the Dharma, then we have to answer in terms of that which contributes to the attainment of liberation. In actual practice, however, you have to proceed in a gradual manner. Even if your aim is to attain liberation, in the beginning of the path—as Aryadeva points out in his *Four Hundred*—you have to stop nonvirtuous action. Before you can actually counter the underlying afflictions, you need to address the behavioral expressions or manifestations of these afflictions. These are the negative and destructive actions of body, speech, and mind. So it is important to abstain from the ten nonvirtuous actions.[93] Within the Buddha's formulation of the ethical discipline of abstaining from these ten actions, the main principle is to address the consequences of anger and hatred so as to avoid harming others. The practitioner of small capacity does not attempt to challenge the afflictions themselves, but addresses the behavioral expressions and manifestations of these afflictions.

Then, as Aryadeva's *Four Hundred* points out, in the middle portion of the path one needs to stop grasping at self.[94] The person of medium capacity targets and works to eliminate the afflictions themselves.

Then, at the third level, Aryadeva says that we must bring an end to all distorted views. This indicates that the person of great capacity is overcoming not only the afflictions but also very subtle residual propensities based on the afflictions having previously been present in their minds. In this way you can connect Aryadeva's three stages of practice to Atisha's three capacities of persons.

The Sequence of Practice

There is a definite sequence to the teachings and practices for persons of the three capacities. You cannot jump to the practices associated with medium capacity or great capacity without laying a foundation by doing the practices associated with a person of small capacity. Engaging in such practice, you turn away from obsessive concerns about this life and move toward concern for future lives.

Then on the next level, reflecting deeply upon the nature of suffering in cyclic existence, you can also turn away from attachment to and preoccupation with future lives as well. Giving up obsessive preoccupation with this life and with future lives, you have a deep sense of disenchantment towards cyclic existence as a whole and a genuine yearning or aspiration to gain freedom.

You then shift the focus, extending that same understanding to other living beings. As you become compassionate toward them, you intensify and extend that compassion to all beings, practicing as a being of great capacity. So the sequence of practices is determined by the stages through which our minds progress as they are transformed.

The stages of the path teachings benefit practitioners at any level of capacity. Within these teachings, you find appropriate practices for your particular mental inclination and spiritual motivation. If you are a person of small capacity, mainly wanting to avoid suffering in a bad rebirth, then there is a way to practice the Dharma within the framework of the four noble truths. In that case, the noble truth of suffering refers to evident suffering, particularly of an intense form, as found in the unfortunate realms of existence. The origins of such suffering include nonvirtuous actions that involve inflicting harm on others. The afflictions behind these actions are the specific forms of the three poisons that are associated with nonvirtuous actions: covetousness, malice, and wrong views.[95] The equivalent of true paths would be adopting the ethical discipline of abstaining from these ten nonvirtuous actions. The equivalent of true cessation would be the temporary freedom of attaining a fortunate rebirth.

So for a person of small capacity, there is an aspiration to find freedom—freedom from unfortunate rebirth. And there are complete presentations of all the practices you need to realize that aim. Thus, in the stages of the path approach, the sufferings of the lower realms of existence are explained, followed by the practice of taking refuge in the three jewels through which you seek refuge from unfortunate rebirths, and then followed by descriptions of the workings of karma and the practice of abstaining from nonvirtuous actions.

Elsewhere, the elements of practice are divided and sequenced in slightly different ways. For example, Tsong-kha-pa's *Three Principal Aspects of the Path* includes within the practices of a person of small capacity meditation on the preciousness of human existence and reflection on its transient nature.[96] After that, contemplation of karmic cause and effect and reflection on the sufferings of the unfortunate realms are included in the practices of the person of medium capacity. These work as a basis for developing a deep sense of disillusionment about cyclic existence and cultivating true renunciation. Thus, while different approaches divide the elements of the teachings slightly differently, the stages of the path tradition always brings together all of the practices of the three persons.[97] Everything is here.

Beginning the Practice

To make the best use of a human life of leisure and opportunity, we should begin by training our minds in the stages of the path that all three persons share with a person of small capacity. The first of these practices is developing an aspiration and dedication to improve our future lives; to that end, we must meditate on impermanence and death. Impermanence is extremely important in the teaching of the Buddha. For example, if you look at the presentation of the four noble truths, where each of the truths has four characteristics, impermanence is one of the characteristics of true sufferings, the first noble truth. We also speak of the four seals of Buddhist doctrine:

- all conditioned phenomena are impermanent
- all contaminated phenomena are in the nature of suffering
- all phenomena are empty and devoid of self
- nirvana is true peace

Here again, the impermanence of all conditioned phenomena comes first. When the Buddha teaches impermanence in the context of the four noble truths and the four seals, the main thing to understand is *subtle* impermanence, which means momentary change. However, for the person of small capacity, the understanding of impermanence is not always especially subtle; it is at a grosser level, where we consider impermanence as death. In these terms, when the continuity of a particular human life comes to an end, this shows the impermanence of that life. Awareness of death is crucial because remembering death and impermanence counters our habitual tendency to grasp at permanence in our own existence—and all forms of trouble arise from grasping at permanence.

Taking Refuge in the Three Jewels

Having cultivated awareness of death and impermanence, you then reflect on the suffering of the lower realms. But what practices can you do to avoid rebirth in an unfortunate realm? You can take refuge in the three jewels and then, on that basis, learn to live in a way that takes into account karmic cause and effect. Refuge is important because the ethical discipline of avoiding nonvirtue is not, in itself, uniquely Buddhist; it becomes a Buddhist practice when it is founded upon refuge in the three jewels. At the outset, and even later in terms of some of the particulars, faith plays a role in developing conviction in karmic cause and effect.

Tsong-kha-pa (1: 178) explains refuge in the three jewels by identifying the conditions for the person seeking refuge, who or what is worthy of being an object of refuge, the manner of seeking refuge, the precepts that you must observe when taking refuge, and the benefits of taking refuge. In effect, he seems to take for granted that the practitioner is already a Buddhist. Refuge is always presented this way in the stages of the path literature.

There are, however, other approaches. The second chapter of Dharmakirti's *Commentary on the Compendium of Valid Cognition* gives arguments to establish the possibility of attaining liberation.[98] The possibility of liberation is also addressed in Chandrakirti's *Clear Words* as it comments on the twenty-fourth chapter of Nagarjuna's *Fundamental Wisdom of the Middle Way.*[99] Nagarjuna presents an objection from a Buddhist realist who feels that if everything is devoid of inherent existence, then cause-and-effect relationships will be impossible. This makes the Dharma untenable, and without the Dharma there can be no spiritual community and no Buddha. The Buddhist realist thinks that if things are empty, the three jewels will be untenable because everything that involves cause-effect relations will break down.

In response, Nagarjuna turns the tables, arguing that if things did have inherent existence, if things were not empty, then it is just *that* situation that would make causal relations untenable. If emptiness is not tenable, then dependent origination becomes untenable, and if dependent origination becomes untenable, then cessation and the path leading to cessation will become untenable. This is because emptiness is not mere nothingness or nonexistence, but rather the absence of inherent nature, the lack of existing by way of some intrinsic character. Without emptiness, things would be only self-instituting; there would be no possibility of interdependent relationships. Connections such as that between the practice of the path and the attainment of cessation would not operate. Chandrakirti's *Clear Words* presents these arguments brilliantly. For those who seek to take refuge, I think it may be very helpful to understand at least some aspects of this.

Selflessness and Liberation

A common question is: If there is no inherently existing self, what transmigrates? Part of the problem comes from an incomplete understanding of the teaching of selflessness. The Buddha does not reject the existence of a personal self. There *is* a person who acts, amassing karma. There *is* a person who experiences the consequences of those actions. The Buddha asks us to analyze the nature of our self. The self, or the person, exists in dependence upon certain physical and mental elements. However, in our naïve perception of ourselves we tend to assume that the self is something like a master that rules over our body and mind, that it is an essence somehow independent of them. It is *that* kind of self, one that we falsely assume to exist, that the Buddha negates. Buddhists refute not the person, but a mistaken conception about the self.

When we Buddhists present the teaching on emptiness, we use the fact that things arise in dependence upon other factors, that things are dependently designated, as evidence that things are empty of their own intrinsic existence. The very fact that we use dependent origination to demonstrate emptiness shows that we do accept some type of existence.

Taking refuge in the three jewels thus requires some understanding of the possibility of true cessations in general—and particularly for oneself. Is it possible for my mental pollutants, the afflictions associated with my mind, to be dissolved and cleansed within the very nature of the mind itself? In order to understand how this is possible, it is indispensable to have some understanding of emptiness.

Moreover, afflictions are origins of suffering, but if our understanding is deep, then we know that there is a fundamental ignorance at the root of the afflictions. And as I mentioned earlier, your view of ultimate reality determines how you define this fundamental ignorance. To have a deeper understanding of the afflictions, down to the subtle level of ignorance, requires some understanding of the way things actually do exist, the nature of reality. Similarly, true sufferings can be understood at a subtle level only with some understanding of emptiness.[100]

Emptiness and Refuge

Ideally, then, some understanding of emptiness is important when taking refuge in the three jewels. For example, when we say, "I go for refuge to the Buddha," the Sanskrit term *buddha* has two different senses. It can mean cleansing away faults or pollutants, but it also suggests flourishing, unfolding like the blossoming of lotus petals. In the Tibetan these two aspects are combined, and the composite term is pronounced *sang gyay* (*sangs rgyas*). *Sang* (*sangs*) means "to be awakened" or "to be cleansed," while *gyay* (*rgyas*) means "to blossom" or "to flourish." Likewise, the Sanskrit term for enlightenment, *bodhi*, is translated into Tibetan as *jang chup* (*byang chub*), where again both meanings of the term are brought into a single composite term.[101]

At the level of buddhahood the total cleansing of all faults and the total perfection of all enlightened qualities is simultaneous, but along the way it is a process of eliminating obscurations. This is because a buddha's enlightened mental quality, a buddha's way of apprehending the world, is—in a sense—naturally present in our minds. It is not something new that we need to create afresh. The practice of the path involves removing obstacles that obscure the expression of our natural capacity to know things as they are. As long as these obstacles remain, they cloud the mind and prevent the awakening of its natural quality. Therefore, in *sang gyay*, the Tibetan word for *buddha*, the syllable *sang*—"cleansed"—is placed first and *gyay*—"flourishing"—comes second.

The point is that to really know what it means to go for refuge, you need to understand the objects of refuge; this in turn requires understanding the teaching on emptiness. You have to understand what buddhahood really means and how it is defined in terms of dissolving all pollutants within the nature of mind itself. Without this, you will not understand how enlightenment and its absence, nirvana and cyclic existence, pertain to the basic nature of the mind itself. So understanding emptiness is crucial.

Likewise, when we say, "I go for refuge to the Dharma," the Sanskrit term *dharma* connotes something that holds you or protects you. To understand this fully you have to understand emptiness. And when we take refuge in the spiritual community (*sangha*), the Tibetan term for *sangha* means those who aspire to goodness. Since goodness here means true cessation, you have to understand true cessations and emptiness in order to comprehend the third jewel as an object of refuge.

Before you can really take refuge in the three jewels you also have to understand karma, the relationship of actions and effects. To this end, you have to understand causation because the workings of karma are an instance of causation; karma is part of a very specific kind of causal relation. Karma literally means "action," but as the term is used in Buddhism, karmic action must have an agent with an intention. Karmic cause and effect is a process in which intentional acts create a chain of effects. Principally, here we are concerned with actions that give rise to experiences of pain and pleasure, happiness and suffering. These experiences are mental phenomena, so their main causes must also be mental. The term "karma," then, most particularly refers to a factor associated with the mental state of a person who is acting. Among Buddhist schools, Vaibhashika and Prasangika sometimes also count physical actions themselves as karma, but the other schools identify karma mainly as a mental factor.

CHAPTER EIGHT

Liberation and Love

Afflictions

IN TERMS OF the origins of suffering, the second noble truth, Tsong-kha-pa (1: 298-306) first discussed the afflictions. Broadly, there are ten types of afflictions, five of which directly relate to our view of reality and five of which are classified as nonview afflictions.[102] But in terms of experience, we are all very familiar with afflictions. Asanga defined afflictions as mental states that disturb the mind stream.[103] If we analyze our experience carefully, then I think it is quite clear that most mental disturbance comes from negative mental states that we call afflictions. The afflictions that are not directly view-related are attachment, aversion, and the like. They are emotions, affective states, and so the cognitive element is less prominent. On the other hand, afflictions that relate to the view are mainly cognitive; they are types of afflicted intelligence. View-related afflictions are particularly serious because they are directly associated with false ascertainment, thinking of things as other than the way they are.

Each type of affliction has its own specific set of antidotes presented in the teachings. For example, love is an antidote to aversion, anger, and hatred. If you are afflicted with attachment, particularly in the form of lust, then it is recommended that you meditate on the impurity of the body. However, these antidotes act only to suppress, not to eradicate, the affliction against which they are directed. In the case of view-related afflictions such as doubt and wrong view, given that they are distorted forms of intelligence, their antidotes also must involve the application of intelligence. So the main antidotes to view-related afflictions involve the cultivation of wisdom that sees things as they are. For that reason, these antidotes, when cultivated fully, have the capacity to eradicate, rather than merely suppress, the afflictions.

Chandrakirti makes this point in his *Clear Words*.[104] He says that the sutras present antidotes against the various afflictions, such as attachment and aversion and anger. When you analyze this carefully, you see that that each antidote works only for its respective affliction. For example, meditation on the impurity of the human body will reduce lust, but does not help with anger or aversion. Meditating on loving-kindness works against aversion, anger, and hatred, but is ineffective against attachment. In fact, meditation on the impurity of the human body can sometimes lead to the affliction of aversion in relation to the body. Also, loving-kindness meditation focused upon a specific individual will help with anger, but it can sometimes lead to an increase in afflicted attachment. In contrast to all other cases, the antidote against ignorance and delusion—the wisdom knowing emptiness—is applicable to all afflictions. Chandrakirti says that the antidote for delusion eradicates all afflictions because delusion about how things exist is the very root of all afflictions.

In terms of our own experience, we want to watch and observe the nature of afflictions as they arise. As we do that, let us investigate and take account of how delusion—in the sense of grasping at true existence—serves as their basis. When we have a strong emotion, such as attachment or anger, toward a certain object, then we can notice that underlying our emotional reaction there is an assumption of some kind of solid reality. We presuppose that we are reacting to an independent or truly existing object. If we can use wisdom to reveal the constructed nature of the object or person, then our forceful grip on the object lessens and our sense of mental grasping eases.

In his *Fundamental Wisdom of the Middle Way* Nagarjuna defines intrinsic nature (*svabhava*): "Intrinsic nature is unconstructed and does not rely on something else."[105] When our minds grasp at an object and we have a strong emotional reaction to it, we presume that the object is independent and unconstructed, solid and concrete. The afflictions are undercut when we dismantle and dissolve that apparent solidness and concreteness. The afflictions start to lose their grip. This is why the antidote against delusion is the wisdom realizing dependent origination in terms of emptiness.

A psychoanalyst whom I met a few years ago told me that in his experience, when someone has a sense of hatred for another individual, he or she perceives many negative qualities in the hated person—but 90% of these qualities are mental projections of the person who is experiencing hate. Of course he is not speaking from a Buddhist understanding, but rather as a scientist. Yet this view fits quite well with the fundamental Buddhist understanding wherein emotional afflictions such as attachment and aversion are grounded in a false, distorted way of attending to and understanding the object.

Then Tsong-kha-pa (1: 304-305) explains how these afflictions give rise to volitional actions, that is to say, karma:

> Accordingly, when those who are under the influence of afflicted ignorance and the reifying view of the aggregates become physically, verbally, or mentally involved in nonvirtue such as killing, they accumulate nonmeritorious karma. Those who perform virtuous acts within the desire realm, such as practicing generosity or maintaining ethical discipline, accumulate meritorious karma.

Soon thereafter, Tsong-kha-pa (1: 305-306) continues:

> This being the case, you might not have acquired, through extensive meditative analysis of the faults of cyclic existence, the remedy that eradicates the craving for the wonders of cyclic existence. Also you might not have used discerning wisdom to properly analyze the meaning of selflessness, and might not have become familiar with the two spirits of enlightenment. Under such circumstances, your virtuous

> activities—with some exceptions on account of the power of the field—would constitute typical origins of suffering, and hence would fuel the process of cyclic existence.

This is an important point. We may engage in various virtuous activities such as generosity and the observance of moral restraint. But unless these virtuous activities are complemented or reinforced by one of the three principal elements of the path—true renunciation, understanding of the correct view of emptiness, and the awakening mind—then, with some exceptions, our virtuous activity will be a cause for continued cyclic existence in misery. Tsong-kha-pa refers to exceptions in terms of "the power of the field." Bodhisattvas are a field of merit; they are practitioners who dedicate everything, over an unlimited time frame, to benefit all beings. So any interaction with bodhisattvas—seeing or hearing them, or even reflecting on them—becomes the basis for the creation of merit. It is said that even when someone causes harm to a bodhisattva, the perpetrator of harm is, through that connection, in the long run led to happiness and to the good.

Twelve Links of Dependent Origination

Tsong-kha-pa (1: 315-325) next explains the twelve links of dependent origination. This teaching is, in effect, an elaboration of the Buddha's teachings on the four noble truths wherein two sets of causes and effects are presented. Beginning with ignorance, the Buddha explains how the origins of suffering, including the afflictions and karma, give rise to suffering. An afflictive ignorance gives rise to volitional actions, which lead to the arising of mental and physical aggregates that are the basis for feelings of suffering and pain. With the aggregates come sensory faculties, which give rise to feelings. The cycle culminates in aging and death, including experiences of grief and sorrow. So here, by explicitly presenting in sequence how the origins of suffering give rise to suffering, the Buddha also implicitly presents the reversal of this process, whereby you bring an end to the origin of suffering and thereby end suffering. In this way, the twelve links also teach the cause and effect associated with the process of enlightenment—that is, the truth of the path and the truth of cessation. The Buddha himself emphasized the importance of this teaching. In Vinaya texts, the Buddha advises monks to have a depiction of the wheel of life, illustrating the twelve links of dependent origination, on the wall outside monasteries and temples.

The twelve fall into three main categories. The first, eighth, and the ninth belong to the category of afflictions, while the second and the tenth belong to the category of karma, volitional action. The rest belong to the category of suffering. In this sense, when we speak of suffering, we are not talking only about sensations, but about the true sufferings that are the first noble truth.

Some of the links are called projecting or propelling factors and others are called projected factors. Some links are called actualizing factors and others are called actualized factors. Overall, the presentation of the twelve links explains the temporal sequence through which this life and future lives are connected in the chain of dependent origination. One cycle of twelve links requires at least two lifetimes. More often, there will be a third lifetime in which the one cycle of twelve will finish.[106] The first link in the chain of twelve is ignorance. There are some Buddhist masters who identify ignorance in terms of a mere unknowing, but most Buddhist masters identify it as an active form of mis-knowing, wrong cognition.[107] So ignorance among the twelve links refers to the fundamental ignorance, a mistaken conception of how things exist. Therefore, your idea of exactly what this ignorance conceives depends on how you understand the ultimate nature of reality. Broadly speaking, we can identify two principal types. There is the fundamental ignorance that is a distorted understanding of the nature of reality. Also, there is another type of ignorance that is a distorted understanding of the cause and effect of actions. This latter type is directly associated with the commission of negative actions, while the first type of ignorance is the root cause of cyclic existence as a whole.

The second link, karma, refers to volitional action. Within the third link, consciousness, there are two temporal stages. The first is the causal stage. This refers to the consciousness at the moment immediately after the karmic act has ceased and it is imprinted upon the consciousness. When a new rebirth occurs as a result of that action, the first instance of consciousness is the resultant stage of consciousness. In relation to the third link, Tsong-kha-pa explains that, although in the sutras six classes of consciousness are mentioned, those who accept a foundational consciousness (*alaya*) take this third link to refer to that foundational mind. And if one does not subscribe to the notion of foundational consciousness, then the third link simply refers to a mental consciousness. In any system, it refers to the consciousness that serves as the basis for the imprints of the karma.

The main advocates of a foundational consciousness are those within the Mind-Only School who follow scriptures, including Asanga for example. Asanga presents various arguments to prove the presence of foundational consciousness. The main basis for this claim is that there has to be a stable and morally neutral basis for storing the seeds of the karma. When an advanced bodhisattva enters into an uncontaminated state of nonconceptual wisdom, even at that moment the imprints of some past karma must somehow still be carried on. Since no nonvirtuous states of mind exist at that point, there must be a neutral consciousness that persists, carrying the seeds of karma. The foundational consciousness plays that role. But the driving force behind this conclusion is the assumption that there must be a continuity of consciousness, something that is findable when you search for its essence. They feel that when you search for the true referent of the term "self," there must be some inherently existing thing at the end of this analysis. They posit the foundational consciousness as that basic self, the continuity of a stable, neutral consciousness. Others accept inherent existence but do not accept the notion of a foundational consciousness, so they say that our ordinary mental consciousness is the repository of the karmic seeds, the imprints of past actions.

However, other Buddhist masters reject any notion of intrinsic existence (*svabhava*) and so they reject the whole approach of presupposing the need to find something solid and real when you search for the essence of the person. They say that the only fact that one can refer to as the person is the "mere I," the nominal "I." So, from their point of view, the consciousness at the point when karmic action ceases is imprinted, but this is a temporary repository of that seed. The long-term basis for these imprints is this "mere I."

The fourth link is name and form. The fifth is the sensory basis. The sixth is the contact. The seventh is feeling. I am not going to elaborate on these.

The eighth link is craving and the ninth is grasping. The difference between these two is that craving relates more to internal sensations and experiences whereas the ninth is a form of attachment pertaining more to external objects. The ninth refers to the attachment to the objects that are giving rise to different sensations that we crave. This ninth link has an element of reaching out, wanting and yearning for an object.

The tenth link is potential existence. This is a state in which karma from the past becomes fully activated in two stages. The first stage is the moment before death; the second stage occurs when the person appears in the intermediate state (*bardo*), the transitional state between rebirths. While the second and the tenth links both belong to the class of karma, the tenth is not actually karma because karma means action. The actual action is far in the past. It is over, but it left an imprint, or seed. One can think of the continuum of the karmic potency as the successive stages of this imprint. Or you can think of it as the continuum of the disintegrated state (*zhig pa*) of that past action.[108] Either way, you cannot say that the tenth link is the original action; it is the state in which a karmic imprint has become fully activated. Then, the eleventh link is birth and the twelfth link is aging and death.

The Twelve Links and Cycles of Rebirth

How do the twelve links in the chain of dependent origination work in a single, complete cycle within cyclic existence? Suppose a particular karma projects just one rebirth. Just before that rebirth, the karmic imprint will be activated and its potency brought to completion, so then rebirth takes place and that single cycle of twelve links is finished with aging and death in that life. But sometimes a single karma projects, for example, one hundred lifetimes. In that case, the earlier links will be all the same, but from the tenth link on each of these one hundred births has its own moment of potential existence followed by its own links of birth, aging, and death.

It is certainly possible for there to be a case in which there is the fundamental ignorance, followed by a volitional action—but then before this karma is even activated by craving and grasping, a whole new cycle of twelve links will begin and be completed. That is, new instances of fundamental ignorance give rise to further karma so that many lifetimes can pass prior to the activation of the original karma. Today, from the time we woke up until now when we are listening to teachings, fundamental ignorance may have given rise to many new karmas—each of which is the beginning of a whole cycle of twelve links.

So in this context Tsong-kha-pa (1: 321) writes:

> This being the case, actualization should be understood as follows: nonvirtuous volitional actions motivated by ignorance about karma and its effects deposit latent propensities of bad karma in the consciousness. This makes ready for actualization the group of links for a miserable rebirth that begins with the resultant period consciousness and ends with feeling. Through repeated nurturing by craving and grasping, these latent propensities are empowered, and birth, aging, and so forth will be actualized in subsequent miserable rebirths.
>
> Alternatively, motivated by ignorance about the meaning of selflessness, meritorious volitional actions—such as ethical discipline within the desire realm—or nondiscursive volitional acts—such as the cultivation of meditative serenity within the higher realms—deposit latent propensities of good karma in the consciousness. This makes ready for actualization the

> group of factors beginning with resultant period consciousness and ending with feeling for, respectively, a happy rebirth in the desire realm or a rebirth as a deity in the higher realms.

After he has explained this in detail, Tsong-kha-pa (1: 323) teaches how important it is in practice:

> When you reflect on your wandering in such a way through cyclic existence, the twelve links of dependent origination are the best method for generating disenchantment with cyclic existence. Contemplate your projecting karma, the virtuous and nonvirtuous karma that you have accumulated over countless eons that has neither issued forth fruitions nor has been eradicated by antidotes. When craving and grasping in the present lifetime nurture them, you will wander through happy or miserable realms under their control. Arhats have immeasurable projecting karma that they accumulated when they were ordinary beings, but they are free of cyclic existence because they have no afflictions. Once you have reached a firm conviction about this, you will hold the afflictions to be enemies and will make an effort to eradicate them.

Tsong-kha-pa (1: 323-324) then explains how the practices of the beings of all three capacities can be summed up within reflection on these twelve links:

> With regard to this, the great spiritual friend Pu-chung-wa engaged in mind training based solely on the twelve links of dependent origination and he made the stages of the path simply a reflection on the progression through, and cessation of, these links. That is, he explained that reflection on the progression through, and cessation of, the twelve links of miserable realms is the teaching for persons of small capacity.

> Reflection on the progression through, and cessation of, the twelve links of the happy realms is the teaching for persons of medium capacity. The teaching for persons of great capacity is first to assess their own situation according to these same two practices. They then develop love and compassion for living beings who have been their mothers and who wander through cyclic existence by way of the twelve links. They train themselves in the wish to become a buddha for the sake of these beings and practice the path to this end.

So Tsong-kha-pa shows that the stages of the path teachings, including the beings of the three capacities, can be understood in terms of Pu-chung-wa's teachings on the twelve links.[109]

The Three Higher Trainings

At this point, Tsong-kha-pa (1: 341-353) presents the three higher trainings through which we can gain liberation from cyclic existence—trainings in ethics, meditative stabilization, and wisdom.

The root of cyclic existence is ignorance. In general, the Buddha identified this as grasping at self-existence. In the twelve links, that self-grasping mainly refers to grasping at the self-existence of the *person*. However, according to the Buddhist school that applies critical analysis in the most refined manner, the difference between the selflessness of *persons* and the selflessness of other *phenomena* is simply a question of what basis is being qualified as lacking self-existence. When it comes to the actual content of these two selflessnesses, there is between these two no difference at all in subtlety or profundity.[110] So the root of cyclic existence, this kind of ignorance, is a grasping at true existence, grasping at the inherent existence of something. In the case of grasping at the self-existence of persons, a particular case is our grasping at our own selves as self-existent with the thought, "I am." This view of ourselves as an inherently existent person is called the "view of the perishing aggregates." This is because it actually depends on a deluded idea of our mental and physical parts, our minds and bodies, as inherently real and self-existent.

The antidote to this ignorance must be a state of mind that directly opposes the perspective of this grasping. Dharmakirti teaches that because loving-kindness and similar minds do not directly oppose the perspective of ignorance, they cannot act as an eradicating antidote against ignorance.[111] We need an antidote that directly opposes the perspective of the ignorance. This has to be a wisdom consciousness that knows emptiness, or no-self. This mind views the same things that ignorance regards as inherently real, but it regards them in a manner that is diametrically opposed to how ignorance sees them. This is the antidote that we need to develop. Therefore, among the three higher trainings, the principal path to liberation is really the path of wisdom.

And yet, to be effective as an antidote, it is not enough to have any sort of mind knowing emptiness. The realization of emptiness has to occur at a very advanced level where there is total clarity. And to know emptiness with total clarity, in a nonconceptual manner, you must have special insight (*vipashyana*) in relation to emptiness. This is possible only if you attain a certain physical and mental suppleness and bliss that arises on the basis of close analysis. But to get to that point you first need a basis, a foundation, which is mental serenity (*shamatha*), wherein you have suppleness and bliss arising from one-pointed mental focus. In this way the attainment of mental serenity is indispensable. And so the training that develops that, the training in meditative stabilization, is essential for the path to liberation.

This training in meditative stabilization involves freedom from various internal distractions. It is really a function of the application of mindfulness and a vigilant meta-awareness, or introspective awareness. Refining and applying these two faculties leads to the attainment of meditative serenity. So you have to start by cultivating the capacities to be mindful and to monitor your own mental states. You can do this by observing sound ethical discipline. You learn to apply the faculties of mindfulness and introspective vigilance with respect to one's own physical, verbal, and mental behavior. At first you learn to set aside external, gross types of distractions; eventually you can also turn away from internal distractions as well. Therefore, the first training, the higher training in ethical discipline, is also essential. All three higher trainings are indispensable to the path through which we seek liberation from cyclic existence.

The Person of Great Capacity

Tsong-kha-pa (2: 15) then introduces the practices of a being of great capacity:

> Therefore, the Mahayana is the origin of all that is good for oneself and others. It is medicine that alleviates all troubles; the great path traveled by all knowledgeable persons; nourishment for all beings who see, hear, remember, and come into contact with it; and that which has the great skill-in-means that engages you in others' welfare and thereby indirectly achieves your own welfare in its entirety. One who enters it thinks, "Wonderful! I have found what I am looking for." Enter this supreme vehicle with all of the heroic strength that you have.

These words are really powerful. Tsong-kha-pa describes the Mahayana as the source of all goodness for oneself and others, the medicine that wards off harm for all beings, and the great path that has been traversed by all the great beings. This accords with Shantideva's *Engaging in the Bodhisattva Deeds:*

> Mounting the horse of the spirit of enlightenment,
> Which dispels all depression and exhaustion,
> And riding from joy to joy—
> What sensible person would ever be discouraged?[112]

And there is a prayer related to the bodhisattva Maitreya:

> Turning us away from the path to the lower realms,
> It shows us the way to the higher realms,
> And then leads us to where there is no old age and death:
> To this spirit of enlightenment, in homage, I bow!

The primary and final purpose of the practice of the mind of enlightenment is to attain buddhahood for the benefit of all beings. However, these verses make the point that if you engage fully in the practice of the spirit of enlightenment, *bodhichitta*, then all of these other aspirations—to avoid bad rebirth, to attain good rebirth, and to attain liberation—can be fulfilled in the process, moving from joy to joy.

At the same time, we have to recognize that there is no way to leap right into the practice of the spirit of enlightenment without actually working through the practices shared with beings of medium and small capacity. The spirit of enlightenment is a mental state involving two aspirations: to attain buddhahood and to bring about the welfare of other living beings. The aspiration to bring about others' welfare requires deep love and compassion, and this in turn requires the attainment of true renunciation. Renunciation, a determination to attain freedom from cyclic rebirth, requires at the outset that you turn away from excessive attachment to this life. So we cannot just jump into practicing only the spirit of enlightenment while ignoring the practices associated with beings of small and medium capacity. As we develop our minds, there is a sequence and a progression. Tsong-kha-pa does not describe the stages of the path for beings of small and medium capacity as something existing apart from the practices of a bodhisattva. Instead, he characterizes these as practices *shared* with the person of small capacity and practices *shared* with the person of medium capacity. For a bodhisattva practitioner whose aim is engage in the distinctive practices of a person of great capacity, all of these other practices are necessary preliminary stages.

Questions for the Dalai Lama

Question: Your Holiness, please tell us more about how the world's religions can exist in harmony. Can this harmony exist only if we all agree that all religions ultimately lead their followers to the same place?

Answer: If by "same place" we mean heaven or liberation from cyclic existence, then that is difficult. There are a lot of differences about such matters. Still, broadly speaking, all major religious traditions have the same purpose. If you seriously practice your own tradition, you come to understand that it is about making the mind more compassionate. A Muslim friend told me, "If you are a genuine practitioner of Islam, then as much as you extend your love to God, to Allah, so also you should extend your love to all creatures." In Buddhism we speak of "mother beings," regarding all living beings as being as dear to us as our own mother. This naturally leads to greater happiness in society. In this way, all traditions have the same potential, the same aim. But as for what happens after this life, they do have different views. Some say we go right to heaven, while other say that we stay, for a while, in the coffin. Yet conflict in the name of religion derives in most cases not from religion itself, but from political ambition, economic interests, or even individual personal interests. Some have manipulated religion to serve these other interests. In other cases there are sincere practitioners who take their religious practice seriously, but hold to the idea that their religion is the only truth. On that basis they think that other religions are not genuine religions. Out of misguided compassion they deliberately destroy those who follow other religions. Certainly that was a problem in the past.

For an individual practitioner the notion of a unique truth that is found through one's own religion is very important. I am a Buddhist and I find the Buddhist approach most effective; for me Buddhism is the best way to transform a negative mind. For another person, however, the concept of a Christian God is the most powerful and for that person Christianity is best; they may feel that the only final truth is in that religion.

We cannot say in general what medicine is best. Each medicine is best for a different illness. Likewise, for those who have certain mental dispositions, Christianity is best. For others it is Islam or Buddhism. In each case, a unique truth found in that one religion is the most effective *for them.*

The truth is that when we consider just the people in this room, there are already many faiths. There are Jews and Buddhists, Muslims and Christians. Each has a different idea of truth associated with his or her faith. We need to recognize the fact that pluralism, the idea of many religions living together, is getting stronger. This is a healthy sign. It is possible for us to live together in peace, but we need more effort in that direction.

Question: Your Holiness, with regard to the three persons of different scope—small, medium, and great capacity—how does one know at what level one's own capacity is? Is this an innate capacity, or is it influenced by an individual's practice, commitment, or desire?

Answer: Tsong-kha-pa's text (1: 139) explains that if you understand these different levels, then you can avoid the arrogant error of thinking you have great capacity when in fact you do not even have the motivation of a practitioner of small capacity.

In the 1960s I had a friend, a British woman, who dreamed of various bodhisattva images; she certainly was having very unusual dreams. She also knew that there are texts that say that one indication of reaching the first bodhisattva level is visions of buddhas and bodhisattvas. So she told me that she had reached that level. Since the texts also say that one cannot completely know another person's level of realization, I did not want to be too blunt with her. I just pointed out to her that the indications of someone having reached that level include other signs as well, such as the buddha fields being shaken and so forth. Even in the case of superior cognition that directly perceives another person's mind, one usually cannot know with assurance another person's level of realization.

In the end, your capacity is something that is attested to within your own personal experience. If you still have strong attachment to money, fame, food, and a comfortable life, then you have not yet reached the level of a practitioner of small capacity. If you find that you are very attached to concerns about your next life and you harbor some admiration for the wonders of cyclic existence, then you haven't reached the level of medium capacity. Examine your own way of thinking and you will know your capacity.

Question: Can one be a practicing Buddhist and still be an active participant in the American system of materialistic rewards and career advancement? These sometimes seem to be a contradiction.

Answer: It really depends upon your state of mind and attitude. If you are mainly motivated to bring about others' welfare, to work for others' benefit, then the many resources of this society can help you fulfill that aspiration. If we consider what Tsong-kha-pa's text (1: 118-120) says about the preciousness of human existence in general, we can see that our particular human lives have many extraordinary characteristics that give us power and opportunity.

Question: How does one find a teacher who has the qualities that Tsong-kha-pa describes? Does that teacher need to be a monk or a nun on the path? What if teachers are far away? Does one need to move, or can one get intense learning from a teacher at a distance?

Answer: This reminds me of a story. When the Kadampa master Drom-don-pa was dying, he lay with his head on the lap of Potowa, his student. Potowa wept and a teardrop fell on Drom-don-pa's cheek. Drom-don-pa looked up asked, "Why are you crying?" And Potowa said, "Up to now you have been my teacher. I have had someone to counsel me and answer my questions. Now that you are dying I will have no one to rely on, so I am sad." And Drom-don-pa answered, "Yes, up to now I have been your teacher, but from now on you should make the texts your spiritual teacher."

This is a beautiful instruction. There is no need to be physically near a teacher; you can seek counsel from the texts. If it becomes necessary to get clarifications of certain points of practice, then you can discuss these with someone. But you do not immediately have to relate to that person as a spiritual teacher. Think of the person instead as a Dharma colleague.

On the other hand, if you want to take vows or a Vajrayana empowerment, then you have to consider your guide as a spiritual teacher. In that case it is very important first to examine whether that person is qualified. The Buddha says that the bodhisattva's compassionate qualities can be inferred by observing behavioral expressions. So observe how the guide behaves, how she or he speaks. It is not a matter of just checking on the person once or twice. Some tantric texts suggest that, if necessary, you should take twelve years to evaluate a teacher.

The teacher must be on the path, but does not have to be a monastic. Geshe Pabongka Rinpoche said that if you are capable you can find liberation even while remaining a householder; but if you are not, then even if you stay in the wilderness meditating, you may actually be creating causes for rebirth in unfortunate realms.[113]

Question: In Buddhism we speak of "sentient beings." Does this include only mammals or does it include insects? Where is the line between what is a sentient being and what is not a sentient being?

Answer: The determination is based on whether there is the capacity to experience suffering and happiness. Many years ago Francisco Varela, the late Chilean scientist, was part of the discussion about what can be empirically identified as a sentient being. In the end there was a consensus that sentient beings include all organisms that are self-propelling, that have the ability to move through space from one point to another according to their preference. We decided that an amoeba is a sentient being. So mosquitoes and bedbugs are certainly sentient beings and we should respect them. It is true that sometimes when we are having a peaceful sleep and a mosquito comes, we might forget that it is a sentient being!

Question: In our country many schools focus time, energy, and personal staff exclusively on teaching the intellect. How can we encourage and instill the seeds of compassion and wisdom in our children?

Answer: This is a vital matter. Professors and scientists have for several years been in serious discussion about how to teach students, from kindergarten up to university level, a sort of secular ethics.[114] This is so important. It is something we are really lacking. Knowledge alone, with no sense of responsibility and no sense of compassion, can be destructive. This is very clear. And there is a limit to how effective external laws, rules, and guidelines can be in restraining this harm. The key is self-discipline, an internal sense of responsibility based on compassion.

Question: Your Holiness, how is it that there are more and more people on the planet if we have all been here since beginningless time?

Answer: Remember that in the Buddhist understanding there are many world systems. So there are sentient beings in other world systems as well.

Question: Could a buddha or a bodhisattva appear as a regular person, just an ordinary person such as one of us, one of the laypersons in the audience? Or must a buddha or bodhisattva manifest as an individual who is found as a reincarnate lama or someone who becomes a monastic?

Answer: The external manifestations of the buddhas and bodhisattvas can be of many different kinds, including animals, so there is no fixed appearance. The Tibetan term "lama" (*bla ma*) translates the Sanskrit term "guru." Etymologically it refers to someone who is unsurpassed. It means unsurpassed in terms of knowledge, in terms of understanding, in terms of realization. The word "lama" does not imply a concept of a living buddha. "Lama" actually means a teacher, so it is a relative term; it makes sense only in relation to a student. When there is a student, there is a teacher. Unfortunately, within Tibetan society the term acquired a different meaning associated with social hierarchy, and we ended up having lama households in which there were so-called lamas but no students.

Therefore, I point out that, when the terms are properly employed, there can be four permutations in the relationship between being a "lama" and being a "tulku" (*sprul sku*). A tulku is a recognized reincarnation of a past holy person. One could be both a lama (a teacher) and a tulku. Or one could a tulku but not a lama, or a lama who is not a tulku. And of course, one could be neither.

Question: Your Holiness, how can a person achieve inner peace when he or she is sensitive and compassionate concerning the suffering and pain of other human beings?

Answer: Shantideva's *Engaging in the Bodhisattva Deeds* raises this question. When you cultivate compassion, you take on additional suffering and pain and that creates disturbance within your mind. Shantideva acknowledges that in compassionately feeling someone's pain you do experience a sense of disequilibrium or disturbance inside you, but he says that this is qualitatively different from our experience of our own pain.[115]

When you experience your own suffering there is an element of involuntariness and lack of control. The pain you feel for others due to compassion has a different aspect because you have chosen to share this pain and it has a dimension of wisdom. In the case of our own pain there is a greater tendency toward fear and insecurity. Whereas when we allow ourselves to share in the pain of others, this may actually increase courage instead of fear. Also, some scientific studies suggest that when someone deliberately cultivates compassion, there is activity in regions of the brain associated with motor activity. This seems to suggest that this practice is associated with a willingness, an inclination, to reach out and do something.

Question: In what language should one say Buddhist prayers? Sometimes I feel so lost when trying to say my prayers in Tibetan. I feel that when I use English it reaches my heart with a clearer intent and understanding.

Answer: It's much better to use the language you know. Tibetans say Sanskrit words without knowing what they are saying. It is much better for them to recite in Tibetan so that they get the meaning. So similarly, for Buddhists who speak English or French or German, it is much better to use one's own language.

CHAPTER NINE

The Spirit of Enlightenment

TODAY WE ARE going to talk about the spirit of enlightenment and helping others. All religious traditions stress altruism in one way or another. What is unique about Buddhism is how this involves the concept of interdependency, dependent arising.

In our daily lives, whether we are religious or not, it is certain that a disposition to help others is the very basis of our well-being—including our physical well-being. We can develop concern for others only on the basis of self-confidence, not out of fear. Increasing self-confidence diminishes fear and gives us a greater sense of inner strength, so that even the physical elements of our body function better. When we are constantly fearful, or angry, or full of hate, then the physical elements are disturbed. This is why, even in terms of physical well-being, an altruistic mind helps—particularly when you are passing through a difficult period. Grounded in self-confidence, an altruistic attitude really gives you sustained peace of mind, a calm mind.

This concept of interdependence is also very helpful in daily life because the reality is that everything is interdependent. Whether we consider economics, ecology, health, or even politics and international relations, everything is deeply interdependent. This is the reality of how things are, but when we find something appealing or threatening it often *appears* to us as though it were independent and isolated. When we act on the basis of such appearances, then our approach is unrealistic. So many unwanted things happen precisely because of this kind of unrealistic approach. Our approach becomes more realistic as we gain fuller knowledge of interdependency. So the Buddhist concept of interdependence gives us a more holistic approach, a more realistic attitude. This is always useful.

Spirit of Enlightenment

Just what is the spirit of enlightenment, *bodhichitta*? Tsong-kha-pa regards it as a mental state in which, motivated by an aspiration to bring about the welfare of others, one aspires to attain buddhahood. This is what we need to develop.

The spirit of enlightenment is sometimes differentiated into four types in terms of the corresponding levels of the path or into twenty-two types, each characterized by a different metaphor. However, most important is the distinction between the aspirational spirit of enlightenment and the engaged spirit of enlightenment. When we ask how these two main types are distinguished, we find slight differences among the explanations of the classical Indian texts. Tsong-kha-pa's understanding is as follows. When a practitioner cultivating the spirit of enlightenment reaches an uncontrived single-pointed aspiration to attain buddhahood for the benefit of all beings, this individual has attained the aspirational spirit of enlightenment. When a practitioner further cultivates a commitment to putting this aspiration in practice, commits to engaging in the bodhisattva practices, and takes the bodhisattva vows, then from that point onwards her or his spirit of enlightenment is an engaged spirit of enlightenment. Tsong-kha-pa (2: 49) bases this interpretation on the first of Kamalashila's *Stages of Meditation* texts. Kamalashila seems to have written the *Stages of Meditation*—unlike his other works—while he was living in Tibet.

Compassion and Suffering

In a sense, having the spirit of enlightenment means having a good heart. But it is not a state of mind that you can generate on the basis of just yearning for others' happiness and yearning to overcome their suffering. Rather, you have to develop it on the basis of a conviction that it is *possible* to achieve happiness and stop suffering. Motivated by that knowledge, you can develop a deep aspiration to bring about others' welfare in the most effective manner. That path involves both wisdom and compassion. Some texts suggest that, within the spirit of enlightenment, compassion brings the welfare of living beings into focus, while wisdom is directed at the attainment of perfect enlightenment.

Having reflected upon the benefits of generating the spirit of enlightenment (2: 16-21), Tsong-kha-pa goes on to explain the actual process by which this mind is generated. And here the principal element really is the cultivation of compassion (2: 28-33). For example, Maitreya's *Ornament for the Mahayana Sutras* explains that compassion is the root of the spirit of enlightenment.[116]

What is compassion? It involves two main aspects: a sense of affection that holds other living beings as dear and a sense of concern for the suffering of those beings. Thus, developing compassion involves cultivating a sense of affection for others along with a wish to relieve their suffering. It is crucial to have a deep understanding of the suffering from which we wish all living beings to be free. We discussed the nature of suffering above in the presentation of the practices relevant to the paths of persons of small capacity and intermediate capacity.[117] The person of small capacity focuses on the nature of evident suffering, everyday suffering such as physical sensations. The practices associated with the person of intermediate capacity involve understanding the nature of suffering at the second and the third levels—that is, the suffering of change and, more importantly, the suffering of pervasive conditioning. Having contemplated the nature of suffering in these profound terms, the person of intermediate capacity develops a genuine aspiration to seek liberation from suffering. This is true renunciation.

When you have personal experience of this genuine aspiration to attain freedom from suffering and you then extend that sense to *other* suffering beings, deep compassion arises. Tsong-kha-pa shows (2: 24) that Maitreya's *Ornament of Clear Realization* defines the spirit of enlightenment as an aspiration to enlightenment for the sake of other living beings, for the welfare of others. The *welfare* of other beings here refers to their *attainment of liberation.*

Compassion is a state of mind in which you aspire for other living beings to be free from suffering; the more deeply you understand the nature of suffering, the more effective that aspiration will be. If your understanding of the suffering of pervasive conditioning is profound, then you will have a strong recognition of the destructive nature of the afflictions that are the root of this suffering. As you recognize more deeply the destructive nature of the afflictions, you will aspire not only to be free from the afflictions, but free also from all latent propensities created by these afflictions. It is these subtle propensities that block attainment of a buddha's omniscient mind.

Two Approaches to the Spirit of Enlightenment

How do we develop the capacity to hold other living beings as dear? How do we cultivate a sense of connection with and affection for them? Historically, there came to be two main approaches: the seven-point cause-and-effect approach and the method of equalizing and exchanging self and others. These two methods derive from different lineages: the seven-point method stems from the lineage of Maitreya, while the equalizing and exchanging method stems from Nagarjuna. Nagarjuna's *Precious Garland* and especially his *Essay on the Spirit of Enlightenment* explicitly teach equalizing and exchanging self and others. We call this the lineage of practices resembling great waves because it teaches an approach most suited to practitioners of high caliber, advanced practitioners.

In the seven-point cause-and-effect method, the key element is to cultivate a sense of other living beings as related to you—as your mother in another lifetime and in other ways—and then build the remaining practices on that basis. In contrast, the equalizing and exchanging self and others does not require considering others as somehow related to you; instead it requires you to recognize the fundamental equality of yourself and others both in terms of aspiration for happiness and in other ways. Shantideva's *Engaging in the Bodhisattva Deeds* says that you should practice the "secret instruction" of exchanging self and others. This wording suggests the need for greater intelligence in this approach.[118]

You use reasoning to establish the fundamental equality of self and other. Establishing this equality is the most crucial step. In this method, from the outset your compassion is not contingent upon recognition of other beings as your family members and so forth. You can recognize the kindness of all other beings—even, for example, an enemy whose hostility gives you an opportunity to advance your spiritual growth. In fact, other beings' appearance as related or unrelated, their behavior and apparent motivations, are not really relevant. You connect with them at a fundamental level, recognizing that just as you wish to be happy and free from suffering, so too do they. Your perspective on them does not depend upon their behavior toward you.

By contrast, the seven-point method begins with the cultivation of recognition of all beings as having been one's mother and reflection upon their kindness. So in this sense the seven-point approach still involves relating to other living beings on the basis of their attitude or their behavior toward you.

In more general talks, I often speak of the difference between ordinary compassion and more developed, genuine compassion. Ordinary compassion is driven by our perception of how others treat us and how they seem to feel towards us. Thus, we can extend ordinary compassion only to friends and family members who seem to care about us. On the other hand, genuine compassion connects to others at a fundamental level. It involves relating to other persons *as* persons, considering, "Just as I wish to be happy, so too he or she wishes to be happy."

The Seven Cause-and-Effect Precepts

Compassion is the heart of the seven-point method. We can think of the other steps as conditions leading up to compassion and then the results of compassion.

You begin by cultivating impartiality (2: 36-37). This is a balance in your feelings towards others such that there is no bias, no sense of discriminating between some who are close and others who are distant.

You then cultivate recognition of all other living beings as dear to you. To do this, you consider the person who is most dear to you in this life—your mother or someone else—and then try to view all other beings in that same light. On that basis, you then cultivate recognition of their kindness, and then the wish to repay their kindness. You cultivate an affection that holds other beings as dear, which leads to compassion (2: 38-47). This compassion culminates in wholehearted resolve, a sublime commitment to free all beings from suffering and provide them with happiness. What is critical is developing this altruistic resolve wherein you assume definite personal responsibility for bringing about the welfare of others (2: 47-48).

Then, ask yourself, "How can I bring about the welfare of others? How can I make this real?" When you consider your current capacity to help others, you see that it is limited. If you cannot take care of yourself, then it is going to be very difficult to help others. There is a Tibetan saying, "Fallen to the ground, you can't help others stand up." Your ultimate aim is to bring about others' welfare, but as a means to that end you will have to attain enlightenment.

But is this possible? It is not adequate to proceed on the basis of a naïve assumption that enlightenment is possible. You need real conviction that enlightenment can arise within your own mental stream. Getting this conviction requires deep analysis. First, you have to see that it is possible to attain liberation. You have to arrive at a conviction that the afflictions can be ended, that there is true cessation. Then, by extension, you will have to recognize that even the subtle propensities induced by these afflictions can be cleared away. This is how you come to know that you really can attain buddhahood.

My own feeling is that a deep understanding of the possibility of perfect enlightenment requires the perspective of highest yoga tantra. This allows us to see consciousness as having many different levels; we can see that complete omniscience is possible on the basis of the very subtlest level of consciousness. The Mahayana presentation of buddhahood in terms of four embodiments[119] really becomes clear when we consider it in terms of the highest yoga tantra teaching on the fundamental, innate mind of clear light. Without that perspective, I think that the concept of buddhahood in terms of four embodiments is rather vague.

Here we see why it is said that in developing the spirit of enlightenment wisdom is what is directed at enlightenment. Above we discussed Nagarjuna's statement that "By means of emptiness the conceptualizations are calmed," which can also be read, "Within emptiness, false conceptualizations are dissolved and calmed." When you really know what liberation and enlightenment are, then, wishing to bring about others' welfare, you can develop the spirit of enlightenment, a genuine aspiration to attain enlightenment.

Exchanging Self and Other

In this practice, you first cultivate a strong sense of the equality of self and others; you then contemplate the disadvantages of self-cherishing and then the advantages of cherishing others and working for their welfare. On that basis you engage in the actual training in exchanging self and others. You then follow this by practicing the meditation called "giving and taking" (*tonglen*). The source for this is Shantideva's *Engaging in the Bodhisattva Deeds*, which, I am told, can be dated to the eighth century. We are now in the twenty-first century and to this day, as far as the cultivation of this exchanging of self and others is concerned, Shantideva's eighth-century text still remains the most excellent. When this mental training leads to some genuine personal experience, then in order to stabilize that realization you take part in a ceremony to confirm this generation of the spirit of enlightenment.

Adopting the Spirit of Enlightenment

Today, we will have the ceremony for adopting the spirit of enlightenment.

In the *Heart Sutra* the Buddha says that all the buddhas of the past, all the buddhas of the present, and all the buddhas of the future attained or will attain enlightenment by engaging in perfection of wisdom practices.[120] So we know that sutra itself says that it is the perfection of wisdom that will lead one to the full attainment of buddhahood. The perfection of wisdom is a direct realization of emptiness wherein wisdom is complemented by the spirit of enlightenment. So we cannot attain buddhahood without the spirit of enlightenment; it is crucial. The wisdom knowing emptiness is a common cause for the attainment of all three types of enlightenment: enlightenment of the disciples, the enlightenment of the self-enlightened ones, and the perfect enlightenment of buddhahood.[121] However, the spirit of enlightenment is the distinctive condition for the attainment of buddhahood. You *must* have it, along with wisdom, to become a buddha (2: 18-19).

Most of us have some conceptual understanding of the spirit of enlightenment. Let us now bring that idea to mind and develop some feeling along with it. When we have a real feeling, an experience that arises from the concept, then we can develop that further and further. One method to confirm your aspiration to enlightenment is to participate in a rite that stabilizes it, allowing it to take hold in the mind. In his *Great Treatise* (2: 61-68) Tsong-kha-pa presents this ritual in a fairly extensive form, as it appears in Asanga's *Bodhisattva Levels.* Since not all of us have that text with us, we will do the ceremony by reciting the three stanzas that I normally use.

Preparing

First, visualize before you the Buddha Shakyamuni, as a living person, surrounded by bodhisattvas. The bodhisattvas appear in the form of deities such as Avalokiteshvara, Manjushri, Maitreya, and Samantabhadra. Then, it is most important to visualize all of the great Nalanda masters, including Nagarjuna, Asanga, Aryadeva, and Vasubandhu. Imagine there with Nagarjuna his precious texts that we can still study and contemplate, along with those of Asanga. This brings it to life. Then visualize Shantarakshita, Kamalashila, and the teachers in that lineage, as well as the great Tibetan masters who succeeded them. Our

Chinese brothers and sisters will visualize their own lineage, as will the Japanese and the Vietnamese, all ultimately the same lineage coming from the Buddha through Nagarjuna. For Theravada practitioners, the lineage comes from the Buddha through Kashyapa, Subhuti, and Ananda, the main disciples of the Buddha.

Then do the seven branches of worship.[122] First, recall and bring to mind all of the enlightened qualities of the body, speech, and mind of the entire assembly of refuge that you are visualizing, especially the qualities of the Buddha Shakyamuni. Reflect on these qualities, especially the quality of having the spirit of enlightenment—a mind that cherishes others' welfare above one's own—and the complementary quality of having direct knowledge of emptiness, the ultimate mode of being of all phenomena. The beings you have visualized embody wisdom imbued with the essence of compassion. As you bring these qualities to mind, make prostrations to the assembly.

Then make offerings. Imagine yourself making offerings to the assembly you have visualized. Offer everything that you own as well as everything else in the world that is not someone else's property. Offer your entire being to the service of all the buddhas and bodhisattvas, beings who from the outset dedicated their lives to bringing about the welfare of an infinite number of living beings. Offer yourself, resolving within, "I offer myself so that I may contribute to the fulfillment of the aspirations of these buddhas and bodhisattvas." Also, imagine offering to all the buddhas and bodhisattvas any virtuous activities that you may have done. Especially offer any virtue that you may have developed on the basis of even the slightest understanding of the concept of the spirit of enlightenment or emptiness. This is the most important offering. Offer your own practice and your own realization.

Next, declare and purify all actions you may have done that have harmed other living beings. Especially confess actions motivated by self-centeredness, an attitude that ignores the welfare and interests of other living beings. Obliviousness to others' welfare can lead to all kinds of harmful activities. Declare these actions and purify them from the depths of your heart.

Then, bring to mind all of the wonderful, enlightened qualities of the body, speech, and mind of the buddhas and bodhisattvas. Cultivate a deep sense of admiration towards them. Rejoice in and admire the virtuous and wholesome things that other living beings are doing and have done, including the loving-kindness, compassion, and altruistic actions of both Buddhists and non-Buddhists. Also, recall the virtuous actions that you yourself have carried out either as a result of cultivating loving-kindness or the spirit of enlightenment, or after meditating on emptiness, or else as a preliminary to these. Bringing to mind all of the virtues of body, speech, and mind that you may have, cultivate a deep sense of rejoicing in them.

Then ask the buddhas and the bodhisattvas—particularly the buddhas—to turn the wheel of Dharma, teaching in accordance with the needs and mental dispositions and capacities of diverse living beings. Appeal to the buddhas not to enter into a final nirvana, but to remain present.

Finally, dedicate all of your merits and virtuous karma towards the attainment of buddhahood for the sake of all beings. Practice the seven branches of worship in this way.

The Actual Ceremony

To begin the actual ceremony for generating the spirit of enlightenment, bring to mind and contemplate what Shantideva says in his *Engaging in the Bodhisattva Deeds*:

> Whatever happiness there is in the world
> Comes from wishing for others' happiness.
> Whatever problems there are in the world
> Come from self-centered desire.
>
> What else is there to say?
> Just look at the difference between
> Ordinary beings who cherish their own welfare
> And the Sage who acts for the welfare of others.[123]

To summarize, Shantideva then says:

> If you do not genuinely exchange
> Your own happiness for others' suffering,
> You will not achieve buddhahood
> And even in this world will find no joy.

Whether we consider our ultimate goal, nirvana, or just our everyday existence, the most precious thing in the world is this jewel-like spirit of enlightenment. It is something that only those with human intelligence can really develop—and right now we have a human life. So resolve to make your human life purposeful, meaningful. There is no more effective way to do this than cultivating the spirit of enlightenment. Shantideva's *Engaging in the Bodhisattva Deeds* says that the buddhas who have contemplated for many eons have found that this is the most beneficial thing to do.[124]

Now, form a clear determination that from now on you are going to practice this attitude of helping others. Based on that attitude, whenever it is possible, help others; when it is not possible to help, then at least restrain from harming them. Be determined to do this not only in this life, but life after life, from eon to eon. Think, "I am determined to keep practicing in this way."

I myself do this practice as much as I can. It really brings me immense delight, immense happiness. It gives so much inner strength. And this is the very best kind of offering to the Buddha. It is not an offering just to the Buddha, but an offering to all living beings.

Now, let us read these three stanzas together, reciting them three times:

> With a wish to free all beings
> I shall always go for refuge
> To the Buddha, Dharma, and Sangha
> Until I reach full enlightenment.

Enthused by wisdom and compassion,
Today in the Buddha's presence
I generate the spirit of enlightenment
For the benefit of all living beings.

As long as space remains,
As long as living beings remain,
Until then may I too remain
To dispel the miseries of the world.[125]

Immediately upon generating the spirit of enlightenment in this way, Shantideva says:

Today my life has meaning.
Having reached human existence,
I have now been born in the family of the buddhas.
I have become a child of the buddhas.[126]

And he adds:

From now on I shall only take actions
That are suited to this family.
Never will I disgrace or pollute
This pure and noble lineage.

CHAPTER TEN

Compassion in Action

Merit and Wisdom

AFTER GENERATING the spirit of enlightenment, you then take up the actual bodhisattva practices. Bodhisattvas aspire to attain a buddha's omniscient state. As we discussed, this is something that arises from causes and conditions.[127] But we need a complete and correct set of causes and conditions, a set that includes many different practices. Nagarjuna summarizes them in the dedication verse of his *Sixty Stanzas of Reasoning*: "May, through this virtue, all beings gather the two collections and on that basis attain the two embodiments of buddhahood."[128] He identifies the collections of merit and wisdom as the causes of buddhahood; when we detail what this involves, we have the teaching of the six perfections. Also, if we further elaborate the sixth perfection, the perfection of wisdom, then we have four additional perfections, making ten altogether.

Explaining the practice of the six perfections, Tsong-kha-pa (2: 85) teaches that we must train in the six perfections after developing the spirit of enlightenment. We cannot become buddhas through either method or wisdom alone. We need both aspects of the path; it is only through joining these two aspects that it is possible to accumulate the causes and conditions necessary for the attainment of omniscient buddhahood.

Among the six perfections, for those pertaining mainly to the method side of the path—generosity, ethical discipline, etc.—the core is practical development and deepening of our wish, our aspiration, to help others. In the case of generosity, for example, the actual act of giving is important, but what is crucial is the strengthening of one's motivation, intention, and inclination to give. The main faculty you are using and thus strengthening is a type of *aspiration*. At the same time, for these method aspects of the path to be effective, you also need the faculty of wisdom because it brings into your practice a sense of conviction or certainty that greatly enhances your practice of generosity, etc.

Likewise, the wisdom aspect of the path has to be complemented by the method aspect of the path. For example, in order to know emptiness, we have to make our minds and hearts receptive to such realization. To do this, you have to engage in practices that purify your mind and strengthen your virtue. In these ways, the two aspects of the path—method and wisdom—really complement each other. Each reinforces and enhances the development of the other. The method side helps the practitioner prepare to realize emptiness and then enhances that realization after it arises. In particular, the method aspect of the path ensures that one's wisdom knowing emptiness can become a powerful antidote to subtle obscurations preventing omniscience and can thus serve as a cause of a buddha's perfect enlightenment. When you consider how bodhisattvas progress from level to level, the actual progression occurs during meditative equipoise on emptiness. So it is the quality of this wisdom that determines how far one can advance; in this sense, wisdom is the principal cause and method complements it.[129]

Six Perfections

In explaining the six perfections, Tsong-kha-pa (2: 104-111) discusses in detail why they are definitely and exactly *six* in number. When a text describes a certain division as being fixed or determinate, we have to consider that this can be meant in more than one sense. For example, the two truths—conventional and ultimate—is an utterly exhaustive division of all objects of knowledge; the number is actually fixed and it is exhaustive. But in a case like the four noble truths, then the determinate status of the number four relates to the very specific purpose of the teaching. It is a fixed number in that context, for a specific purpose. My sense is that the definite enumeration of the perfections as six is similar. It is not an exhaustive list, like the two truths. It is a number that is fixed, but is fixed just in relation to the particular purposes of a specific teaching. Sometimes a teacher finds that a fixed list with a determinate number of items is most effective in dispelling certain misunderstandings.

Generosity

The first of the six perfections is generosity. Tsong-kha-pa (2: 113-126) gives a straightforward explanation of this very important topic. We need to reflect upon this and put the teaching into practice.

The critical point is to be sure that your giving will benefit others. To that end, we have to consider what it is appropriate to give, when to give, and so forth. Tsong-kha-pa (2: 122) lists three main forms of giving: giving of material things, giving protection from fear, and giving the Dharma through spiritual teachings. For example, if you are careful that your motivation is correct, then working to protect the environment can be an instance of the second type of giving, giving protection. The work of those in the caring professions, including doctors and nurses, can also become a form of giving protection from fear.

When professors and teachers give lectures, this might be a form of generosity, giving spiritual teachings. But if their motivation is just to get the pay, then it is not actually generosity. It is a business transaction like any other business. Even if the Dalai Lama gives a lecture for the purpose of getting some money, then that is just a business deal, not a form of generosity. There once was a Nyingma master who made three pledges: never to ride any animal, never to eat meat, and never to take any material offerings given as a result of his Dharma teachings. He explained that taking money for giving Dharma teachings was just doing business—a bad kind of business. Traditionally, selling the Dharma has been considered the very worst sort of business.

Ethical Discipline

Tsong-kha-pa (2: 148) explains that the second perfection—the perfection of ethical discipline—is of three main types: restraining oneself from harmful actions, gathering virtue, and working for others' welfare. There is a natural sequence among these three, progressing from restraining oneself, through gathering virtue, and then to working for others.

If a bodhisattva has vows of individual liberation, such as lay or monastic vows, then the observance of those vows constitutes the first type of ethical discipline, the ethics of restraint. When a bodhisattva has no formal vows, then the ethical discipline of restraint means abstaining from the ten nonvirtuous actions.[130] It also includes guarding against self-cherishing thoughts. Restraining yourself from harmful actions will prepare you to develop a virtuous heart.

Gathering virtue, the second type of ethical discipline, can include all the practices that lead to the development of the many aspects of the path, including both practices related to the profound emptiness and the vast practices of compassion and skillful means. As your mind becomes strong in virtue, you will be better able to bring about the welfare of others.

In explaining the ethical discipline of working for the welfare of others, Tsong-kha-pa (2: 148) mentions eleven forms of service. He does not detail them here in his *Great Treatise*, but refers us to his *Basic Path to Awakening*, which comments on the ethical discipline chapter of Asanga's *Bodhisattva Levels.* There he teaches that we should respond when someone needs help. For example, if someone has trouble walking, then just help that person. Help others when they are confused or ignorant about a particular task they are trying to do. Go out of your way to reach out to others, welcoming them and so forth. Stand by those who are in difficulty and afraid, giving them companionship. Support and comfort those who are suffering in grief and sorrow. Respond with help to those who have immediate material needs. Be a refuge, a shelter, for those in need of emotional support. Take care that, in trying to help others, whatever you do is done in a manner that is attuned to their states of mind and thus can actually bring benefit. If someone seems to be headed down the wrong path, counsel that person so as to gently steer him or her toward virtue. When necessary, take a firm stand—especially when it involves harm being committed by someone else. And if, some day far in the future, you develop extraordinary powers through meditation, then use these powers to help others.

Patience

As for the third perfection, patience, Tsong-kha-pa (2: 159) explains that there are three main types: patience that disregards harm that is done to you, patience in enduring hardship and pain, and patience that is a kind of certitude about the various aspects of the Dharma. This section of the *Great Treatise* (2: 151-179) cites and derives mainly from the wonderful explanations in the sixth chapter of Shantideva's *Engaging in the Bodhisattva Deeds.*

Joyous Perseverance

Tsong-kha-pa's *Great Treatise* (2: 181-207) explains the fourth perfection, joyous perseverance, based mainly on the seventh chapter of Shantideva's *Engaging in the Bodhisattva Deeds.* He (2: 184) identifies three forms of joyous perseverance: armorlike joyous perseverance, joyous perseverance of gathering virtue, and joyous perseverance of working for the benefit of other living beings.

Armorlike joyous perseverance requires cultivating an attitude that takes into account an extremely long time frame. It means developing the feeling, "Even for the benefit of a single living being, I shall dedicate myself for eons, as long as space remains." For example, the Panchen Lama's *Offerings to the Guru* says, "I will strive for the welfare of others, even for the sake of a single living being; even if I must remain in the lower realms for eons, I shall not be disheartened." This long-term, resolute determination is really what qualifies joyous perseverance as "armorlike."

Meditative Stabilization

Tsong-kha-pa explains the fifth perfection, the perfection of meditative stabilization, and the sixth perfection, the perfection of wisdom, in the latter portions of the *Great Treatise* under the headings of "serenity" and "insight," respectively. In the most general sense, serenity (*shamatha*) and insight (*vipashyana*) are practices common to the Buddhist and non-Buddhist traditions of classical India.

In the *Descent into Lanka Sutra* the Buddha teaches a spiritual pluralism that identifies many vehicles or methods for proceeding on a spiritual path, including the vehicle of the humans, the vehicle of Brahma, the vehicle of the disciples, and the vehicle of the bodhisattvas. As long as there exists among living beings such tremendous diversity of mental dispositions and spiritual inclinations, there will be a need for tremendously diverse forms of practice. The human vehicle refers to any system in which the primary purpose is progress on a path leading to freedom from immediate and evident suffering. But the Brahma vehicle mainly focuses on dispelling the suffering of change; at this point serenity and insight become very relevant. The main idea is to advance through various levels of concentration and formless states of meditative absorption. Although based upon cultivation of meditative serenity, the actual path involves insight that compares the characteristics of the lower realms with the progressively subtler character of the higher realms.

How can we be sure about the existence of the three realms—the desire realm, the form realm, and the formless realm? We can get some understanding by examining our own mental states. Mental states pertaining to the desire realm are quite gross, so they have coarser forms of the afflictions and other mental processes. On the other hand, if you attain mental stabilization, then you can stay in a relatively stable state of mind. And among meditative states, you will find progressively deeper, subtler states. Accordingly, you can infer that there might also be *realms*, states of being, which correspond to and are the karmic outcomes of these different mental states. This is one way to get a sense of the existence of the three realms.

In his *Songs of Spiritual Experience* Tsong-kha-pa says that serenity constitutes mastery or dominion over one's own mind. Serenity has a kinglike quality in the sense that when you direct the mind to a chosen object, it stays right there with the solidity of a mountain. On the other hand, you can also use this power to analyze any virtuous object you might choose. In that case you would be developing the faculty of insight on the basis of serenity. Serenity provides mental stability and insight provides an analytical capacity. These two can come together.

Moreover, Tsong-kha-pa says that meditative stabilization produces bliss as your body and mind become supple. This refers to the attainment of physical and mental pliancy, a gradual thinning of our natural inertia. Yogis who are cultivating serenity use this pliancy to demolish any hindrance or distraction and maintain meditative stabilization. I know a monk who studied in the scholastic monasteries and mastered the classical Buddhist texts, but also did many years of meditation. He lived in Bhutan for a while, cultivating serenity, and he reached a point where his experience was permeated by a sense of bliss. I think he had attained this bliss derived from physical and mental pliancy.

The Perfection of Wisdom

In Buddhism generally, the term "wisdom" can pertain both to facts about conventional reality and to facts about ultimate reality. In the context of education, "wisdom" refers to a faculty of intelligence that must be developed. Or it can refer to learning. The Tibetan classical tradition naturally follows the model of classical Indian Buddhist tradition wherein there are five main fields of knowledge and five secondary fields of knowledge. The five principal fields of knowledge are the study of grammar (mainly Sanskrit), the study of logic and epistemology, medicine, arts and crafts, and systematic Buddhist knowledge. The minor fields of knowledge include many other similar topics. In the classical

Indian Buddhist model, these were regarded as the key domains within which the educated person should cultivate wisdom.

When we speak of the perfection of wisdom, however, "wisdom" refers to knowledge of ultimate reality, the ultimate nature of things. In his *Songs of Spiritual Experience* Tsong-kha-pa says that wisdom is the eye with which one sees the profound reality. Wisdom is the path by which one eradicates, destroys from the very root, the basis of cyclic existence. The root of cyclic existence is delusion, particularly in the form of grasping at true existence, and wisdom knowing emptiness works as a direct antidote opposing the perspective of this fundamental delusion, thereby destroying it. Tsong-kha-pa says that, for this reason, wisdom is the most precious treasure of all the marvelous virtues described in all of the scriptures.

All the teachings of the Buddha, either directly or indirectly, converge upon the teaching on emptiness. They may be pointing toward emptiness, they may be actually leading to emptiness, or they may be actually settled upon emptiness. So Tsong-kha-pa, in his *Praise to the Buddha for Teaching Dependent Origination*, addressed the Buddha, "Everything that you teach proceeds from dependent arising for the sake of nirvana, so you have nothing that does not lead to peace." Tsong-kha-pa then goes on to say that the wisdom understanding this is like a wonderful light that dispels the darkness of delusion.[131]

Attracting Others

Tsong-kha-pa's explanation of the practices of the bodhisattva path, besides the six perfections, also covers (2: 225-231) four main ways to gather followers: (1) giving people things that they need, (2) speaking in a beautiful way, (3) leading others to practice virtue and work toward liberation, and (4) living your own life in accordance with the Dharma. This last point is important: Whatever you teach others, you must set an example by your own practice.

CHAPTER ELEVEN

Serenity

Becoming an Object of Refuge

AS BUDDHISTS we go for refuge to the three jewels. We say, "I go for refuge to the Buddha, I go for refuge to the Dharma, I go for refuge to the Sangha." When we speak of the three jewels—the Buddha, the Dharma, and the Sangha—as objects of refuge, they can be causal objects of refuge or resultant objects of refuge. That is to say, our purpose in taking refuge in the Buddha, in praying to the Buddha, is to bring about a certain result. We will *become* buddhas. Our final destination is buddhahood. At the same time, we have right now the seed of buddhahood, a subtle mind that is empty of any independent existence. That very nature is the basis for all mental transformation. This is what makes it possible to eliminate wrong views.

In order to achieve buddhahood we first need a spiritual community; we must take refuge in a Sangha. But what qualifies someone as truly a member of the Sangha? Truly to be a member of the Sangha in which we take refuge requires the presence of the true Dharma within one's mind. And Dharma here means a true cessation, a nirvana, and the path leading to it. You become a member of the Sangha when you actualize the path within yourself.

Of course, in the beginning, as a causal object of refuge, the spiritual community, or Sangha, refers to beings who still have more to learn, those who are still in training. You attain the stage of no-more-learning only when you become fully enlightened. As for resultant objects of refuge, Maitreya's *Sublime Continuum* points out that the Buddha can be seen as the embodiment of all three jewels—the Buddha, the Dharma, and the Sangha.[132]

How do we get from here to buddhahood? There is the famous mantra from the *Heart Sutra*: *Gate gate paragate parasamgate bodhi svaha* [Gone, gone, gone beyond, gone completely beyond, enlightenment!] That is it, that is the way. As a joke, I tell people that *gate gate paragate parasamgate bodhi svaha* is also the meaning of our *physical* life. We are first children, then young adults, then we reach middle age and later old age. In this case, *svaha*, the last word, means death. Physically, our final destination is the cemetery. Perhaps I have already attained the fourth level (old age), while others of you here are at the second and third levels. But there is nothing sacred in this, nothing liberating.

Therefore, *gate gate paragate parasamgate bodhi svaha* must pertain to *mind* rather than body. It is about the transformation of the ordinary minds we now have. We always want to be happy and we always want to overcome suffering. But the seeds of suffering are within us. And the root source of all of these problems is right here. We have to identify and eliminate this source. It is possible even within this lifetime to gain some experience of this if you experiment with practice in a serious way. And this experience will give you a real conviction, a sense of certainty that liberation is really possible. *Gate gate paragate parasamgate bodhi svaha*. We *can* free our minds.

Serenity and Insight

For this ordinary mind to advance to progressively higher states we have to cultivate a union of serenity and insight. The final section of Tsong-kha-pa's *Great Treatise on the Stages of the Path to Enlightenment* explains this, opening with the salutation (3: 13), "I pay respectful homage at the feet of those Venerable Masters who are the embodiments of great compassion." Tsong-kha-pa then states that he is going to explain how to train in the last two perfections—meditative stabilization and wisdom—by cultivating serenity and insight.

Earlier we saw that the heart of the path to liberation is the practice of the three higher trainings in ethics, meditation, and wisdom. Cultivating serenity belongs to the higher training in meditation, while cultivating insight belongs to the higher training in wisdom. However, when we explain these in terms of a bodhisattva's practice, we present the path in terms of the six perfections.[133] Here the cultivation of serenity and insight belongs to the last two perfections.

To cultivate serenity and insight is to bring out and strengthen faculties that are naturally present within your mind. If you closely observe your own mental states, you will see that there is a certain quality within your mind that enables you to focus on a chosen object and to maintain attention. This is concentration, the basis of meditative stabilization and insight. You also have the ability to discern and to differentiate various characteristics of a chosen object. This aspect of your mind is the faculty of intelligence or wisdom, the basis for insight. We have to develop these natural faculties; we have to *perfect* them.

Cultivating serenity means developing the natural faculty that enables us to keep our attention on a chosen object. We have to apply *effort*; we have to persevere with enthusiasm in strengthening that particular quality of our mind. As we make ourselves more familiar with and habituated to it, our minds are enhanced. The quality of mind that allows us to focus, to maintain attention, is a conditioned phenomenon. The more we cultivate the causes and conditions that give rise to it, the more effective and powerful it will become. In actual practice, we have to constantly apply the faculties of mindfulness (*dranpa*) and also vigilance (*shayshin*), the latter being a monitoring awareness or "meta-awareness" that watches for any distraction or deficiency in the quality of our attention. But in order to do this, we have to remove obstacles that interfere with our cultivation of serenity. We have to set up the right conditions for the practice.

Preconditions for Meditative Serenity

Asanga's *Levels of Hearers* lists thirteen preconditions for the cultivation of serenity; Kamalashila's second *Stages of Meditation* distills these into a list of six.[134] Tsong-kha-pa's *Great Treatise* (3: 28-30) directs readers to Asanga's text, but presents the six from Kamalashila, including finding an appropriate place to practice, minimizing craving, and so forth. Asanga's list includes four practices that Tsong-kha-pa's *Great Treatise* (1: 100-108) already explained in the section on what to do between meditative sessions. These involve maintaining appropriate diet and sleeping patterns, restraining the senses, and acting in the world with careful self-awareness.

Posture

Tsong-kha-pa (3: 31) then explains how to take up an appropriate physical posture. In the practice of serenity our main aim is to develop and to enhance single-pointed attention; to this end our physical posture is crucial. For example, if you practice while lying down, this tends to bring your mind into a relaxed, lazy state. So it is better to practice upright. We sometimes speak of the seven-point Vairochana posture as an appropriate posture. When you add in a point of instruction on breathing, it is called the eight-point posture of Vairochana.[135]

Your legs can be either completely crossed or else half-crossed, as you would normally sit. Either way, you need to adopt a posture that does not put too much strain on your knees. Otherwise, you will lose your focus. Position your hands in the gesture of meditation, with your left palm underneath and your right palm on top of it. If you are doing Vajrayana practice, then it is better to have your thumbs touching each other so that they form a triangle. Your arms should not be touching your sides, but rather slightly outstretched so that they also form a natural triangle. Your spine should be straight as an arrow. Rest your teeth naturally; don't grit your teeth. (If you happen to have no teeth, this will not be a problem!) Your lips also should rest in a natural position. Don't force anything.

Your tongue should be slightly curved and touching the roof of your upper palate. If you happen to enter a deep meditative state, this posture will protect you from having saliva dripping down. Also, this tongue position tends to soften your breathing and prevents your mouth from getting too dry.

Position your head so that it is just slightly bent. Keep your eyes slightly downcast and focused on the tip of your nose. If you happen to have a rather large nose, then you won't have a problem because you will see the tip of your nose quite easily. But if you have a rather flat nose, don't try too hard to see the tip of your nose. This will strain your eyes. Instead, just keep them slightly downcast.

Meditate with your eyes slightly open and resting naturally; it is fine if once in a while they naturally ease closed. You are cultivating this meditative state in your *mental* consciousness, not at the level of the sensory experience. As you become familiar with meditation, you will become oblivious to external sensory stimuli, including whatever appears in your field of vision. Tsong-kha-pa here explains eye position in the cultivation of serenity, but in other contexts it varies. For example, in Kalachakra tantric practice we keep the eyes wide open and looking upwards. In Dzogchen, you look straight in front.[136]

Finally, your shoulders should be positioned naturally, but slightly extended. Your breathing should not be too harsh or too slow, but should take place naturally. Tsong-kha-pa (3: 31) describes how to breathe in the context of serenity meditation:

> Your inhalation and exhalation should not be noisy, forced, or uneven; let the breath flow effortlessly, ever so gently, without any sense that you are moving it here or there.

Flawless Concentration

Tsong-kha-pa (3: 33-71) explains how to develop concentration on the basis of Maitreya's *Separation of the Middle from the Extremes.* Maitreya speaks of five flaws or faults and eight antidotes against these faults. The five faults are: (1) laziness, (2) forgetting the object, (3) excitement and laxity, (4) failing to apply the antidotes when excitement or laxity arises, and (5) excessive exertion.

There are eight antidotes to these five faults. For the first fault, laziness, Asanga specifies four antidotes: faith, aspiration, effort, and pliancy. Faith here refers to confidence in the benefits of meditative stabilization, notably physical and mental pliancy. Meditative stabilization makes your mind and body supple and serviceable, fluidly responsive to your will. This benefit arises from any Buddhist or non-Buddhist practice of deep concentration. In the context of the stages of the path, Buddhists cultivate serenity with the ultimate aim of applying it to our understanding of the ultimate nature of reality. Without serenity, insight cannot arise and without insight, there is no liberation. So Buddhist practitioners recognize a special benefit to serenity. Reflecting on these benefits of meditative stabilization fosters faith, a sense of trust in what one is trying to accomplish. Based on this trust, you feel a sense of interest and an aspiration to cultivate that state. This in turn makes you enthusiastic to apply yourself, remedying the flaw of laziness.

For the second fault, forgetting the object of meditation, the main antidote is the cultivation of mindfulness. For the third fault, excitation and laxity, the antidote is vigilance—the monitoring "meta-awareness." For the fourth fault, the failure to apply necessary antidotes when excitation or laxity arises, the antidote is cultivating the intention to apply them. The fifth fault is inappropriate application of exertion or effort. At advanced levels, when your mental stability is very firm, exertion becomes counterproductive to the maintenance of this stability. Here the antidote is cultivating equanimity.

Objects of Meditation

In general, you can choose to meditate on any external or internal phenomena. You can cultivate single-pointed mental focus on a pebble, a twig, or a stick. Or you can meditate on an internal mental state such as a feeling. For example, there are the four foundations of mindfulness: mindfulness of body, feelings, mind, and mental objects. These include both internal and external things as objects of one's meditation.

Tsong-kha-pa (3: 35) tells us that the Buddha identified four types of meditative objects: universal objects, objects for purifying behavior, objects for expertise, and objects for purifying afflictions. Objects of meditation for purifying behavior are those that are particularly appropriate to the experience or emotional temperament of individual practitioners. Due to factors in the past and present, individuals have different temperaments and emotional styles. Considering those differences, you need to choose the particular object that will be most effective. Objects of meditation for expertise pertain to fields of knowledge within which you are cultivating an understanding. The objects may be enumerations such as the five aggregates; you cultivate single-pointed meditative awareness of them.

When we cultivate serenity in meditation, we can choose an external or an internal object of meditation. But even when we take an external object, what we actually focus upon is not the physical thing itself, but rather a mental image of the physical thing. That becomes the object of our concentration. Among internal phenomena, one could learn to meditate on such things as one's channels, drops, or the energy that flows within these channels.[137] A more profound object one can choose is one's own mind. Still more profound than that is choosing emptiness as the object of meditation.

Choosing emptiness as one's object of meditation when cultivating serenity presupposes that you have already realized emptiness. Such a practitioner would have to have gone through a process of analysis and discerned emptiness, attaining a correct view of reality. On that basis, she could take emptiness as an object of meditation, cultivating single-pointedness. This approach is called *seeking meditation on the basis of the view*. It is possible only for a few people whose mental faculties are really advanced. The main approach of Tsong-kha-pa's *Great Treatise* is instead *seeking the view on the basis of meditation*. First we cultivate serenity with regard to some other object. Then we apply analysis to gain realization of emptiness.

Meditating on the Mind

In Mahamudra[138] and Dzogchen we cultivate single-pointed focus with the mind as our object of meditation. When we speak of practices that are shared by sutra and tantra, we do not distinguish levels of subtlety in consciousness. But in the highest yoga tantra, we make these differentiations and we can choose a subtle type of consciousness as the object with regard to which we cultivate serenity.

Here we also have to consider what we mean by the "object" of meditation in different contexts. When you meditate on impermanence or selflessness, clearly you are taking impermanence or selflessness as the object of your meditation, the *content* of your meditation. But we also speak of meditating on compassion, loving-kindness, faith, and devotion. In such a case, you are not taking compassion as the meditative object; rather, you are cultivating compassion within your mind. Like this latter case, when you practice meditation on the nature of the mind at a subtle level, you are in fact cultivating or developing the mind of clear light.[139] So what we refer to as the "object" of meditation can play different roles in the process.

We can practice meditation in which we focus on the mind, taking the mind as our meditative object. However, don't form the impression that a single instant of the mind, a single mental state, somehow looks at itself. That would mean autonomous self-cognition (*rangrig*).[140] We are talking about something less dramatic that operates within a very minute time frame. For example, in one instant there is a mental state that takes as its object the mental state of the immediately preceding instant. In order to do this kind of meditation, cultivating serenity with mind itself as the object, you first must identify the object. That is, you must have some recognition of what mind itself is.

Knowing our own minds is a challenge because in everyday experience our minds are dominated either by external stimuli or internal sensation. Either our mind is directed totally outwards and takes the form of whatever comes into our field of experience or else we experience our mind just in the form of internal sensations. Either way, it seems that the actual nature of the mind itself is obscured. The mind's own flavor, its character as clear and knowing, is hard to catch. You need to find a way to ensure your focus is not swept away by recollections of past experiences or by thoughts projecting into the future—anticipation, hope, etc. You must somehow stay right in the present moment.

We are so habituated to and dominated by looking backward and forward that when we try to stay right in this moment, we experience a kind of emptiness. Of course, this is not emptiness in the philosophical sense. It is a mere absence and, at first, it may be just a fleeting experience. Then, as you familiarize yourself with this practice, you will gradually be able to extend the period of time during which you experience this absence. Identifying your mind so that you can take it as an object of meditation is not an intellectual process; it is a matter requiring actual experience. Eventually, you will be able to experience mind in the form of this absence. Then, from within this, the very nature of the mind—on the conventional level—will become apparent, even obvious.[141] The mind is clear and knowing. You can take that as your object of meditation, cultivating serenity on that basis.

Meditating on an Image of the Buddha

Tsong-kha-pa's *Great Treatise* (3: 43-46) recommends taking an image of the Buddha as your object of meditation. This is easier than meditating on the mind and it has special significance for Buddhist practitioners. Practitioners of other religious traditions can choose an object with special significance to them. A Christian could meditate on an image of Jesus Christ or, perhaps, a cross. Would a Muslim perhaps meditate on the Arabic letters of the name "Allah"?

If you choose the image of the Buddha as an object of meditation, it is helpful to choose a slightly small image. This can have the effect of making your mind more alert. Then, imagine that this image is very bright, like a light. This prevents your mind from sinking into some forms of laxity. Also, imagine that the image is heavy. This will protect you from mental scattering and mental excitation.

Mindfulness and Vigilance

Having chosen an appropriate object, you cultivate meditative serenity by applying and maintaining mindfulness, in a very undistracted manner, so as to develop single-pointed attention. Mindfulness keeps your attention from slipping off the object of focus. However, you have to monitor whether your attention is actually staying on the object of meditation, whether you are becoming distracted or affected by mental laxity. Vigilance plays this monitoring role; it is a sort of "meta-awareness" that tracks whether mental excitation or mental laxity has arisen. Thus, mindfulness means keeping your attention on the chosen object of meditation; vigilance monitors how well you are doing that.

The obstacles that vigilance monitors are mental excitation and laxity. Mental excitation belongs to the family of attachment, desire; it tends to occur readily because of our long habituation to seeking things that attract us. A primary effect of excitation is distraction from the meditative object. It is an indication that your mental state is overstimulated, raised up too high. You need to find a way to calm it, to dampen it down. One antidote would be meditating on impermanence or the suffering of pervasive conditioning. This will have the immediate effect of dampening excitation.

Laxity means that your mind apprehends the meditative object without vividness or alertness. Your mind is dull or downcast rather than lifted up. An antidote that would raise your mind up could be reflecting upon the benefits of cultivating the spirit of enlightenment or the benefits of cultivating the wisdom knowing emptiness. Or you could contemplate the preciousness of this human existence and the opportunities it accords us. These considerations may incite a sense of joy that will raise your state of mind, clearing away laxity.

Breath Meditation

For many of us who are beginners, it may be very beneficial to meditate on the breathing process. As an object of meditation, it is not as subtle as the mind, yet it is subtler than meditating on an external material object. Directing attention to the breath can be a very effective way to develop serenity. You simply place your attention on each inhalation, each exhalation. Keep it focused for one hundred, or one thousand, respirations. My acquaintances who are meditators tell me that when they take breath as the object of their meditation, their minds become really settled if they maintain focus for a period between one hundred and one thousand breaths.

In Vajrayana, there are special breathing practices at the preliminary stage that involve nine rounds of breathing.

In everyday life, breathing meditation can be extremely helpful. If we find our mind in a disturbed, agitated, or irritated state, we can bring down the level of this disturbance simply by drawing our attention to our breath and focusing. This has an immediate effect.

At the same time, remember that breathing meditation is a respite, giving temporary relief. It does not solve the underlying problem that gave rise to our emotional disturbance in the first place. A deeper approach, bringing long-lasting benefit, is to meditate on dependent origination, the interdependence of things. Or we can reflect on impermanence and then cultivate the wisdom knowing emptiness. We can reflect deeply on the benefits of *bodhichitta*, the spirit of enlightenment. Naturally, these will be much more effective and powerful practices.

How Much Should One Meditate?

There is no fixed number of meditative sessions each day, nor is there any fixed length for sessions. In most cases, beginners should keep sessions short but frequent. As you progress, you can keep the high quality that you develop in these short sessions while gradually increasing the length of each session. That is the best approach.

To Serenity and Beyond

If you adopt sessions of the proper length and do the actual practices correctly in sitting meditation, then you will progress through nine stages of mental development,[142] culminating in the attainment of a serenity in which your mind and body are pliant, serviceable, and responsive.

On the basis of serenity, you can cultivate insight. Tsong-kha-pa's *Great Treatise* (3: 91-103) concludes the section on serenity by explaining a *mundane* type of insight that one may cultivate on the basis of serenity. But in the very next section, Tsong-kha-pa will explain why this is inadequate. We must cultivate profound insight into the very nature of things, the ultimate reality.

CHAPTER TWELVE

The Purpose of Emptiness

Serenity Is Not Enough

TSONG-KHA-PA (3: 107) begins his presentation of insight by citing what the Buddha taught in the *King of Concentrations Sutra*:

> Although worldly persons cultivate concentration,
> They do not destroy the notion of self.
> Afflictions return and disturb them,
> As they did Udraka, who cultivated concentration in this way.

There are people who attain serenity and on that basis cultivate a mundane insight that compares the characteristics of this realm, the desire realm, with the characteristics of the higher realms.[143] In this way, they attain the heightened states of mind associated with those higher realms. However, these meditations leave totally intact their grasping at self. And so long as self-grasping remains, there will also be a reified sense of "other." Dharmakirti points this out in his *Commentary on the Compendium of Valid Cognition*: "Where there is self, there will be a notion of the other."[144] This reified differentiation of self and other gives rise to attachment and aversion, which in turn give rise to a whole host of problems.

In a similar vein, Chandrakirti's *Commentary on the Middle Way* says that after grasping at the notion of self or "I," we go on to grasp at things as "mine."[145] We each know from personal experience that this is true. When you grasp at your self, then you grasp at things that belong to you—including your friends and families. The stronger the grasping, the more forcefully it leads you into attachment, aversion, and so on. One insight common to all Buddhist schools is this recognition that grasping at self lies at the root of afflictive mental states such as attachment and aversion.

Mundane insight, although based upon serenity, does not undermine grasping at self, so the person who has attained even such an advanced state is still vulnerable to the afflictions. The *King of Concentrations Sutra* says, "Afflictions return and disturb them." Heightened meditative states suppress gross levels of the afflictions, but because the seeds of these afflictions are still there, the afflictions resurface when conditions are right. The Buddha gives an example: "As they did Udraka, who cultivated concentration in this way." Udraka had been one of the Buddha's teachers.

Tsong-kha-pa (3: 108) then cites the next verse from that same sutra:

> If you analytically discern the lack of self in phenomena
> And if you cultivate that analysis in meditation,
> This will cause the result, attainment of nirvana;
> There is no peace through any other means.[146]

In contrast to someone like Udraka, with only mundane insight, one needs to discern the lack of self in all phenomena. This must be done via critical analysis showing that all phenomena are devoid of existence in their own right, existence by way of their own nature. Then, as one develops familiarity with that understanding in meditation, one comes to ascertain that fact deeply, with a strong sense of conviction. As one internalizes this knowledge of selflessness, one comes to see all phenomena as having an illusionlike quality. Such insight undermines the grasping at self. Grasping at self is a deluded mental state; it is *not* an inseparable essential quality of the mind itself. So it can be removed by gaining insight into the nature of mind. This is how we eliminate pollution from our minds; as the sutra says, this is what leads to nirvana.

Aside from understanding selflessness, are there other gateways leading to liberation? Is there an alternative—a second door or a third door? The Buddha says that "There is no peace through any other means." Dharmakirti's *Commentary on the Compendium of Valid Cognition* points out that loving-kindness and the like do not directly counteract or oppose ignorance, so they cannot eliminate it.[147] This is what the Buddha is telling us in the *King of Concentrations Sutra*. To become a buddha one must cultivate virtues including loving-kindness, but they are no substitute for wisdom knowing emptiness because they do not directly counteract the perspective of self-grasping. Direct knowledge of emptiness is the only antidote powerful enough to eliminate the root of cyclic existence.

Definitive Sources

To cultivate insight in relation to emptiness you first have to understand emptiness. That is, you must comprehend it at an intellectual level before you can have profound meditative certainty about it. So how are we to understand emptiness?

All Buddhist schools share adherence to the four seals of the Buddha's Dharma:

- all conditioned phenomena are impermanent
- all contaminated phenomena are in the nature of suffering
- all phenomena are empty and devoid of self
- nirvana is true peace

But there is divergence as to how to understand the Buddha's teaching on selflessness. The diversity of the Buddha's teachings shows his recognition of the diverse needs of his followers. Nagarjuna's *Fundamental Wisdom of the Middle Way* acknowledges that sometimes the Buddha says that things possess final existence, whereas other times he says that they do not.[148] In his *Seventy Stanzas* Nagarjuna explicitly says that this makes it difficult to fully penetrate the Buddha's way.[149] We have to learn how to discriminate between teachings of the Buddha that can be taken at face value and those that need to be interpreted. That is, we need to differentiate provisional and definitive teachings.

There are sutras where the Buddha says that the mental and physical aggregates are the burden and the one who bears that burden is the carrier. Such passages seem to suggest that over and above the five aggregates there is something else, a carrier that is the person. It is almost as if he is suggesting a real self that is in some manner independent of the five aggregates. Then, there are other sutras where the Buddha says that the person does not exist, but karma exists and the aggregates exist. Yet again, there are sutras where he says that external objects do not exist, but the mind truly exists. And of course, there are sutras in which the Buddha denies true existence across the entire spectrum of phenomena, internal and external. For example, the *Heart Sutra* says that even the five aggregates are devoid of inherent existence. The Perfection of Wisdom sutras teach that all phenomena—from visible forms through the Buddha's omniscient mind—are devoid of intrinsic nature and thus are primordially at peace.

These diverse teachings of the Buddha evolved over time into the diverse positions of Buddhist schools. These schools differ over many matters, including whether one can make distinctions between definitive and provisional teachings. The Vaibhashika school rejects that differentiation, maintaining that all of the Buddha's statements are definitive. Within the Sautrantika school, the Followers of Reasoning subschool appears to accept that there is a need to differentiate definitive and provisional teachings.

Even within the Buddha's own teachings we find systems for interpreting scripture. The *Sutra Unravelling the Intended Meaning*, for example, teaches the three turnings of the wheel of Dharma.[150] In that text the Buddha defines the first turning and the second turning as nondefinitive scriptures and the third turning as definitive. For those who instead accept texts of the second turning as definitive, this might seem to be a problem because it is the Buddha himself who says this. Yet in the *Teachings of Akshayamati Sutra* the Buddha gives very different criteria for what is definitive.[151] Thus, when it comes to determining which sutra is definitive, we cannot rely entirely on scripture because—as we have seen—the scriptures seem to contradict one another.

If scripture itself were our only means to resolve contradictions between scriptures, which scripture would we rely on to guide us in making these determinations? To establish any given sutra as definitive, you would need some other sutra to say that it was. But then you would need another sutra to tell you that *that* sutra was reliable, and so forth. The process of seeking scriptural support would be infinite. Of course, if our teacher, the Buddha, were here right now, then we could ask him—but that option is not available.

In fact, the only way we can differentiate the definitive is by means of reasoning and analysis. Statements in sutra that, upon being subjected to critical analysis, are not contradictory to reason and can be supported by reason—those are definitive. Statements in sutra that, when subject to critical analysis, prove to be untenable and contradictory—these are not definitive, but provisional teachings. This is the only way we can really make the distinction. This is why Nagarjuna composed the six volumes of his Analytic Collections.[152] The collective name given to these six volumes is really beautiful because it emphasizes the role of reasoning, critical analysis. The Buddha himself teaches this:

> O monks, just as a goldsmith tests his gold
> By melting, cutting, and rubbing,
> The wise accept my teachings after full examination
> And not just out of reverence for me.[153]

Don't accept scriptures at face value. Analyze them and accept their validity on the basis of the understanding you thereby develop.

The Buddha's Purpose in Teaching Emptiness

In the twenty-fourth chapter of his *Fundamental Wisdom of the Middle Way* Nagarjuna presents Buddhist essentialists as charging him with nihilism, arguing that the teaching of emptiness implies a rejection of the law of karmic cause and effect. Nagarjuna begins his rebuttal by saying that this charge is brought by those who have failed to understand the purpose and meaning of the Buddha's teaching on emptiness. The purpose is to help eliminate all of our distorted perceptions and distorted states of mind. Buddhist schools join in a consensus that grasping at self is a fundamental distortion, but they characterize selflessness in different ways. Some understand it as the absence of a substantially existing person, a person possessed of some self-sufficient substantial reality. They cultivate wisdom realizing selflessness in that sense. Such realization will have an impact—it will reduce grasping at a gross level, undermining grasping at your own self as substantially real. But it does not affect grasping at the basis of the self, the mental and physical aggregates. So you still have a sense that possessing this basis constitutes your own natural way of being.

Consider how we relate to objects that we find attractive. Even before you buy something in a store, you may already feel attached to it. Yet the quality of attachment really changes after you purchase it. Now you label the object "mine" and you relate to it as "mine." This shows that as long as there is some basis for identifying something as *mine*, grasping at the self as an owner will persist. This is why it is inadequate to realize selflessness only in the sense that the person is devoid of self-sufficient, substantial existence.

To address this, there are Buddhist teachings on selflessness in relation to phenomena *other than the person*. The Chittamatra school, for example, says that the selflessness of phenomena is the absence of subject/object duality. We tend to see objects as true referents of the term that we apply to them; that is, we act as though particular objects naturally existed as objective referents of their names. You can learn to dismantle the apparent solidity of this external reality and then, by meditating upon this, reduce your grasping at external objects.

However, if you don't apply such analysis to your own internal states—your sensations, feelings, and mental states—then there is still a basis for grasping. You may not grasp so obviously at external objects, but you will still grasp at your own subjective experience. Therefore, the Madhyamaka approach negates exaggerated reality across the entire spectrum of phenomena. Nothing has any *true* existence. This means that nothing actually exists in the way it now appears to us.

Within Madhyamaka, there are two principal understandings of emptiness. One still presupposes some degree of objectivity to things, some inherent nature. This is the Svatantrika Madhyamaka approach. It supposes that these phenomena, while existing in relation to our perception, have their own mode of being that can appear to an undistorted mind. Thus, this assumes some kind of objective nature in things themselves.

In contrast, Prasangika Madhyamikas reject even on the conventional level any notion of things' existing objectively, by way of some power from their own side. Svatantrika Madhyamaka leaves a subtle basis for grasping, a degree of objective reality. Nagarjuna's *Sixty Stanzas* points out that mental poisons will continue to arise in any mind that still holds on to an objective basis.[154] This is why Prasangika Madhyamika teachers reject even on the conventional level the notion of objective, inherent existence. They dismantle any basis for objectification. There is no ground, no self-supporting basis—nothing left to be grasped at.

We see a kind of parallel in quantum mechanics.[155] In classical physics it was assumed that objects possess some self-defining or objective reality. The discoveries of quantum mechanics now make it difficult to maintain a classical model of objective reality. There is a growing understanding that the very notion of reality incorporates the idea of some *perspective*, and thus there is some inevitable role for consciousness. I have noticed that in quantum physics there are difficulties articulating what reality is. This is because scientists have come to realize that they cannot ground reality in the objective status of things.

In Prasangika Madhyamaka there is no objective ground or basis for reality. All phenomena are dependently originated. All phenomena exist and are real only in terms of language, terms, and designations. This does *not* mean that anything goes, that anything can be anything. It's not the case that you can just imagine something and that will make it real. Quantum physics has trouble incorporating their new insights while also maintaining the sense that things are real. For Madhyamaka philosophers as well, the crucial challenge is how to maintain that middle way, the perfect balance. We must totally reject any notion of objective or intrinsic reality, yet at the same time accord to things an actual existence that is adequate to account for the working of dependent arising.

As you carefully analyze each of the several explanations of selflessness you will begin to see that there is something incomplete or incorrect in each of the earlier ones. As you gradually progress, your understanding will culminate in the subtle view of the Prasangika Madhyamaka, where intrinsic existence is rejected entirely. When you reach the view that all phenomena are devoid of inherent existence, you will understand that this is something accurate and complete. This is final and definitive. There is no contradiction.

The Madhyamaka Tradition

Tsong-kha-pa (3: 115-117) then explains the history of the various interpretations of Nagarjuna's teachings that evolved in India. How did Madhyamaka evolve? Nagarjuna's followers and interpreters included his own immediate disciple, Aryadeva, as well as Buddhapalita. Those who follow Buddhapalita's reading of Nagarjuna include Chandrakirti and Shantideva. But there evolved another line of interpretation of Nagarjuna and Aryadeva, beginning with Bhavaviveka and including Jñanagarbha and Shantarakshita, along with Shantarakshita's student Kamalashila. So, you have two main strands of interpretation of Nagarjuna's writings. Within the Svatantrika group deriving from Bhavaviveka there are two subdivisions. One accepts the notion of external reality while the other, more in line with the Chittamatra school, denies external reality. Bhavaviveka and Jñanagarbha belong to the first group; Shantarakshita and Kamalashila take a more Chittamatra-like standpoint.

In the *Great Treatise* Tsong-kha-pa mainly presents the Prasangika standpoint of Chandrakirti, rejecting the notion of intrinsic existence even on a conventional level. In the case of the Tibetan tradition, we find that the early translation school of Nyingma, the Mahamudra teaching of the Kagyu school, the union of clarity and emptiness teachings of the Sakya school, as well as Tsong-kha-pa's own Geluk tradition all present their understanding of emptiness from the point of view of the Prasangika. However, the Tibetan tradition also includes the "emptiness of other" standpoint, sometimes called Great Madhyamaka.[156] Some masters of that tradition reject the interpretations of Nagarjuna presented by Buddhapalita and Chandrakirti. They present instead a convergence of the viewpoints of Nagarjuna and Asanga, arguing that Nagarjuna's *Hymn to the Ultimate Expanse* presents Nagarjuna's final position.[157] The teachings found in the *Hymn to the Ultimate Expanse* are very similar to what we find in Maitreya's *Sublime Continuum*.[158]

When you examine the writings of these great masters, naturally there are differences in the terminology they use and the approaches they present. However, when it comes to the final understanding, the Panchen Lama Losang Chogyen's Mahamudra text says that all of the diverse Dharma teachings converge for someone who is learned in definitive teachings, skilled in reasoning, and possessed of profound yogic realization.[159] We must also remember that the teachings of the Tibetan and Indian masters can be framed in terms of two different approaches, one tailored for a specific individual and another approach that teaches in terms of a comprehensive view of the Dharma.[160]

CHAPTER THIRTEEN

Reality and Dependent Arising

IN THE SALUTATION of Nagarjuna's *Fundamental Wisdom of the Middle Way* he characterizes ultimate reality as the total pacification of conceptual elaboration. This is helpful to remember as we consider what Tsong-kha-pa (3: 119) says about the profound reality of things just as they are:

> Nirvana is the reality one seeks to attain, but what is nirvana? If "entry into reality" means a method for attaining it, then how do you enter? The reality that you seek to attain—the embodiment of truth—is the total extinction of conceptions of both the self and that which belongs to the self, specifically by stopping all the various internal and external phenomena from appearing as though they were reality itself—which they are not—along with the latent predispositions for such false appearances.

This is called "nonabiding nirvana." Tsong-kha-pa (3: 119) explains further:

> The stages by which you enter that reality are as follows: First, having contemplated in dismay the faults and disadvantages of cyclic existence, you should develop a wish to be done with it. Then, understanding that you will not overcome it unless you overcome its cause, you research its roots, considering

> what might be the root cause of cyclic existence. You will thereby become certain from the depths of your heart that the reifying view of the perishing aggregates, or ignorance, acts as the root of cyclic existence. You then need to develop a sincere wish to eliminate that.
>
> Next, see that overcoming the reifying view of the perishing aggregates depends upon developing the wisdom that knows that the self, as thus conceived, does not exist. You will then see that you have to refute that self. Be certain in that refutation, relying upon scriptures and lines of reasoning that contradict its existence and prove its nonexistence. This is an indispensable technique for anyone who seeks liberation.

Tsong-kha-pa's explanations here are based on Chandrakirti's *Clear Words*.[161]

The other Madhyamaka school, Svatantrika, adheres to the notion of inherent existence, so for them there is a difference between the selflessness of phenomena and the selflessness of persons, with the former considered more profound. However, in Chandrakirti's Prasangika explanation of emptiness, it is very clear that the selflessness of persons and the selflessness of other phenomena are not at all distinguished in terms of their subtlety or profundity. Tsong-kha-pa (3: 122) cites Nagarjuna's *Precious Garland*:

> As long as you conceive of the aggregates
> You will conceive of them as "I."

In order to realize the selflessness of persons completely, you must also overcome grasping at the true existence of other phenomena, including the mental and physical aggregates.

Aryadeva's *Four Hundred* says that "The seed of cyclic existence lies in consciousness; objects are the field of experience of this consciousness."[162] Seeing the lack of self in these objects ends the seed of cyclic existence, which is really our grasping at the self. To eradicate the very basis of cyclic existence we have to bring about within ourselves a genuine understanding that the self at which we grasp does not in fact exist.

If the self at which we grasp *did* exist, what would it be like? What would be the implications of its existence? We have to use reason to analyze this very critically. To do this we must first identify the manner in which we grasp at this notion of self. This is called identifying the object of negation. Then, through analysis, we can demonstrate that the self at which we grasp does not really exist. When we understand the total nonexistence of this self, then we can take that understanding to heart, familiarize ourselves with it, and gain a strong conviction. This is the only way to eliminate that grasping.

How does the self that is the object of negation relate to our personal experience? We have to examine how the sense of self arises in us naturally. The thought "I am" is a very natural sense of selfhood that we all have. However, if we examine this carefully, we will see that within our core sense of self—especially when the sense of self manifests in a strong form—there is an underlying supposition or assumption that the self somehow exists in between the body and the mind, as something separate from them, over and above them. We feel or assume that what we call "I," the referent of our sense of self, has some kind of concrete reality. It seems to be self-defining, self-sufficient, able to set itself up. And we have that sense not only about ourselves; we relate to everything else in just this same way. When we perceive something externally, we tend to regard that object as if it existed, in its own right, out there where we see it. It seems like something that we can point our finger at and pin down. It seems to occupy a specific space, etc.

When we say that such self-grasping is deluded, we do not mean that the person or that the mental and physical aggregates do not exist. The person exists. We can speak of the person's having a past rebirth and a future rebirth. We can make distinctions between one person and another. The person as a unique individual *does* exist.

What is being negated is the person's existing in the particular manner in which we tend to assume that the person exists. We assume that the person exists as a separate, self-sufficient reality. Even before we think about things, even at the level of sense perception, things appear as solid, concrete realities, things able to exist on their own power. Some Madhyamika teachers do contend that that perception of true existence arises only at the level of thought, not at the level of the sensory experience. But here in Chandrakirti's Prasangika system, what is being negated is very subtle. This subtle sense of inherent existence is already there at the sensory level. Then, based upon that perception, we think of and grasp at things as existing in this way. We affirm in thought what we have perceived, taking things to have whatever kind of reality they seem to have when they appear to our senses. In the case of the person, we appear to ourselves as possessing inherent existence, so we accept and affirm that perception, grasping at it. This grasping conception of *inherent* existence—*not* the mere existence of the person—is what must be refuted. Inherent existence itself, the content of that misconception, needs to be disproven.

The Seventh Dalai Lama writes powerfully on this subject. He says that when our minds are intoxicated with sleep, various events and objects arise in our dreams. Within our dreams, we take things to be real, to exist just as they appear. But in fact nothing that appears in dreams exists as it appears at that time; it is all unreal. Likewise, in our everyday life we are intoxicated by the deep sleep of delusion that grasps at inherent existence, so when things appear to our minds, they seem to have objective, independent reality. However, our perceptions of things as existing in that way are baseless, unfounded. Even though the objects of our senses have no intrinsic reality at all, each object appears to us as though it had a self-instituting, self-defining reality of its own. Because we are under the spell of delusion, it appears to us that things exist in their own right, objectively. The content of this distorted perception is the subtle object of negation. We must refute it comprehensively, without leaving a trace.[163]

Consider also the explanation of Gung-tang Rinpoche. He says that when we cultivate the view of emptiness, we set out to understand the nature of things. In that process, we do not find any inherent existence. This nonfinding of inherent existence in itself constitutes the negation of inherent existence. In general, failing to find something does not prove the nonexistence of that thing. But what about a situation where something should certainly be findable when properly sought, and we then have searched for it scrupulously and failed to find it? In such a case, not finding something entails its nonexistence. Inherent existence is like that. If it were real, we should find it when we search. It is negated when we fail to find it under analysis of the nature of things. Gung-tang then points out that this does not at all imply the nonexistence of the basis upon which you understand emptiness, the things that are empty of inherent existence. The mere existence of things is left untouched. In the aftermath of this analysis, things exist only nominally, as mere designations. On that level of nominal existence, mere conventional existence, we have to be able to posit the workings of cause and effect, etc. That cause and effect exist and function, that relationships still work without inherent existence—this is something you will have to affirm in the light of your personal experience of the world. Gung-tang calls this "arriving at the right point."[164]

We may use Nagarjuna's fivefold reasoning to analyze inherent existence.[165] The person and the aggregates in relation to which it is designated are neither identical nor essentially different. Neither exists as an essential core within the other, and they are not interdependent by way of some essential property or inherent relation. This fivefold analysis becomes a sevenfold analysis if we add the consideration that the person is not the mere collection of the aggregates and is not the shape of that collection.[166] When you subject the personal self as now conceived to that kind of analysis, you do not find it. If you think that the person does exist objectively, you should then be able to say, Is it identical with mental and physical aggregates or is it really separate? Does this objectively real self underlie the aggregates as their support, or vice versa? You won't be able to find the self in any of these ways. This shows that persons do not exist objectively, in their own right.

While objective existence is untenable, subjective reality is also a problem. Can we actually identify the existence of things only in terms of our own personal mental state? When we see that neither subjective existence nor objective existence is tenable, we are left with one alternative: nominal existence. We come to understand that all phenomena exist only in nominal terms.

Avoiding Nihilism

It is very important to identify accurately what it is that we are negating when we analyze the final nature of things. As Tsong-kha-pa (3: 126) says, there are two ways to go wrong here: negating too much and not negating enough. Gung-tang points out that those who negate too much claim to be Madhyamikas while in fact sharing with Buddhist essentialists the premise that if things do not possess inherent existence, then they don't exist at all![167]

The identification of existence with intrinsic existence is the premise of Buddhist essentialists who, in the twenty-fourth chapter of Nagarjuna's *Fundamental Wisdom of the Middle Way*, charge that teaching emptiness implies a rejection of the four noble truths. There have been those who claim to uphold Nagarjuna's emptiness while using the five-fold reasoning to refute existence all together. They actually share with essentialists the premise that any existence at all must be inherent existence. For that perspective, the absence of inherent existence implies the absence of existence.

Those who negate too much include those who think that Nagarjuna's tradition rejects any kind of valid cognition or reliable knowledge. They take Nagarjuna's teaching that everything is mere designation, utterly devoid of inherent nature, to mean that things have no existence. Gung-tang points out that, for them, this will preclude any differentiation between good and bad, right and wrong. None of these distinctions can be maintained. We can understand their perspective because to say that a perception is a reliable source of knowledge, that perception must be nondeceptive regarding its object. It has to be true to how things are. These Madhyamaka interpreters reject this kind of truth in perception; this leads them to reject any notion of valid cognition or reliable knowledge.

However, if you reject all existence and all distinctions along with inherent existence, then nothing will exist. You fall into nihilism and you are not upholding the true middle way—which Nagarjuna defines not as nonexistence, but as emptiness. In terms of the basis, how all things exist, emptiness *is* that fundamental middle way.[168] As the middle way, emptiness must be free from both extremes, the extreme of absolutism and the extreme of nihilism. It is crucial to understand Nagarjuna's teachings on emptiness in this way. Nagarjuna says that the essentialists don't understand emptiness itself, nor the purpose and meaning of the teaching on emptiness.[169]

Nagarjuna does not say that emptiness is total nonexistence or the utter inability to find things when searching for them. Instead, his *Fundamental Wisdom of the Middle Way* identifies emptiness with dependent arising: "That which arises dependently we explain as emptiness."[170] He equates emptiness with dependent origination in the sense that the very meaning of emptiness is dependent origination. This in turn derives from the Buddha's statements "What is arisen from conditions is devoid of arising," and "Such a thing is devoid of any intrinsic arising." The Buddha goes on to say, "Therefore, that which is arisen from conditions is said to be empty."[171] Therefore, in equating emptiness with dependent origination rather than with nonexistence Tsong-kha-pa is following what Nagarjuna and the Buddha taught.

Nagarjuna's *Fundamental Wisdom of the Middle Way* adds that "this is dependent designation and the true middle way."[172] The expression "dependent designation" is very powerful; it includes two elements: dependent and designated. Dependence immediately conveys the idea that phenomena do not have an independent status. They are all contingent upon other things, and those things are in turn dependent on others. The term "dependent" thus negates any notion of inherent existence. The second element, designation, conveys the notion that things are not nothing; things have a conventional identity that emerges from dependent relations. Combining these two elements, the expression "dependent designation" indicates the middle way; Nagarjuna calls it the true middle way.

Thus, the meaning of emptiness must be understood in terms of dependent origination. Dependent origination can be explained in terms of causes and conditions, but also in terms of dependent designation. So Tsong-kha-pa (3: 129) explains:

> This attainment [of buddhahood], as explained earlier, is based on their having amassed along the path immeasurable collections of merit and sublime wisdom, collections within which method and wisdom are inseparable. That, in turn, definitely relies upon attaining certain knowledge of the diversity of phenomena. This profound knowledge understands that the relationship of cause and effect—*conventional* cause and effect—is such that specific beneficial and harmful effects arise from specific causes.

Here Tsong-kha-pa refers to emptiness in terms of cause and effect. With that as a basis, one moves to the second level of understanding dependent arising—dependent designation. And so he (3: 130) writes:

> At the same time, amassing the collections of merit and wisdom also definitely relies on attaining certain knowledge of the real nature of phenomena. This means reaching a profound certainty that all phenomena lack even a particle of essential or intrinsic nature. Certain knowledge of *both* diversity and the real nature is needed because without them it is impossible to practice the whole path, both method and wisdom, from the depths of your heart.
>
> This is the key to the path that leads to the attainment of the two embodiments when the result is reached. Whether you get it right depends upon how you establish your philosophical view of the basic situation. The way to establish that view is to reach certain knowledge of the two truths as I have just explained them. Except for the Madhyamikas, other

> people do not understand how to explain these two truths as noncontradictory; they see them as a mass of contradictions.

Tsong-kha-pa is talking about dependent origination both in terms of cause and effect and in terms of dependent designation. He (3: 130) continues:

> However, experts possessed of subtlety, wisdom, and vast intelligence—experts called Madhyamikas—have used their mastery of techniques for knowing the two truths to establish them without even the slightest trace of contradiction. In this way they reach the final meaning of what the Conqueror [i.e., the Buddha] has taught. This gives them a wonderful respect for our teacher and his teaching. Out of that respect they speak with utter sincerity, raising their voices again and again: "You who are wise, the meaning of emptiness—emptiness of intrinsic existence—is dependent arising. It does not mean that things do not exist, it does not mean that they are empty of the capacity to function."

Dependent Arising and Emptiness

When we say that things are empty, we are negating something. It is very important to identify the object of that negation correctly. If we fail to do this at the outset, then in meditation we may experience some absence or emptiness, but it will not necessarily be the final emptiness. For example, when we meditate on the person's lack of self, we may just assume that we are meditating upon the person's emptiness of inherent existence. In fact, we may only be getting at a coarser emptiness, the negation of a substantially existent person.

We might also veer into a different sort of misunderstanding of emptiness. Nagarjuna's *Fundamental Wisdom of the Middle Way* characterizes emptiness in terms of the total pacification of conceptual elaboration.

On that basis, some understand emptiness as the mere stopping of conceptual thought. We may analyze emptiness in terms of the diamond slivers, looking at how things arise from causes.[173] Or we may rely on the reasoning of the lack of identity or difference, examining the thing itself. But in the end, nothing can be found because when we subject things to this kind of analysis, they are completely unfindable, totally untenable. And some people do take this unfindability to mean that nothing exists or else that no determination at all can be made about things. Even Tsong-kha-pa himself had this view early in his career, when he was composing his *Golden Garland of Eloquence*. And in an early poetic retelling of a bodhisattva story, Tsong-kha-pa says that all things are illusory and unfindable, yet for the sake of others the bodhisattva assumes the validity of dependent origination. In other words, in his early work he seems to take the validity of dependent arising as something to assume only in terms of helping others rather than as something to adopt as one's own view.

But later in his career, in his *Three Principal Aspects of the Path*, Tsong-kha-pa says that as long as unfailing dependent arising (at the level of appearances) and emptiness (at the level of reality) alternate in one's mind like a weaver's feet, never going together, then one has not yet reached the final intention of the Buddha. The convergence of emptiness and dependent arising is the crucial point.[174]

In his *Fundamental Wisdom of the Middle Way* Nagarjuna (24.18) explains that the very meaning of emptiness is the meaning of dependent origination: "That which arises dependently we explain as emptiness." The reasoning of dependent origination—that things are empty because they are dependently originated—does not lead only to a demonstration that nothing can be found under analysis. In this way, it differs from other proofs of emptiness, such as the diamond slivers. Instead, it shows that things emerge only from other things, through dependent relations. For this reason, the argument of dependent origination has the power to transcend both the extreme of absolutism and also the extreme of nihilism or nonexistence.

Nagarjuna's *Precious Garland* makes this even clearer:

> The person is not the earth element, the water element, and so forth. Nor is it the consciousness. In this case, where is the person over and above these elements?[175]

Having raised this question, Nagarjuna does not then immediately give us the conclusion that the person is devoid of inherent existence. He does not jump straight from the analytic unfindability of the person to the conclusion, emptiness. Instead, he provides an intermediate verse indicating that the person exists, not as an ultimate, but in relation to a composite of the elements. In other words, he first shows that the person cannot be found under analysis and *then* brings up dependent origination. Only after that does he return to the analysis and conclude that the person has no final reality.[176] This shows that persons *do* exist, but since this existence is only through dependence, persons have no intrinsic reality of their own. They have no *inherent* existence.

Chandrakirti's *Commentary on the Middle Way* says that a chariot cannot be found, conventionally or ultimately, when subjected to the sevenfold analysis, but that *without* such critical analysis and on the level of worldly convention there is a chariot.[177] A chariot is designated in relation to its various components. Chandrakirti explains that emptiness is the absence of inherent existence; it is the absence of any form of existence that is grounded in its own reality.[178]

Tsong-kha-pa's *Great Treatise* (3: 132) says:

> The twenty-sixth chapter of Nagarjuna's *Fundamental Wisdom* teaches the stages of production in the forward progression of the twelve factors of dependent arising and the stages of their cessation in the reverse progression. The other twenty-five chapters mainly refute intrinsic existence.

This is the reason that, when I teach Nagarjuna's *Fundamental Wisdom*, I begin with the twenty-sixth chapter. This chapter uses the twelve links to teach dependent arising in terms of cause and effect. This provides a basis for understanding cause and effect and at the same time provides the basis upon which emptiness can be established. This approach is in the spirit of Nagarjuna himself, whose *Fundamental Wisdom* says, "Without relying on the conventional, the ultimate cannot be made known."[179] Chandrakirti's *Commentary on the Middle Way* likewise states, "The conventional is the means and the ultimate is arrived at through that means."[180] When you understand dependent arising, you use that as a premise upon which to base your analysis of the emptiness of inherent existence.

The *Great Treatise* (3: 132) says:

> The twenty-fourth chapter of Nagarjuna's *Fundamental Wisdom* analyzes the four noble truths. It demonstrates at length that none of the teachings about cyclic existence and nirvana—arising, disintegration, etc.—make sense without emptiness of intrinsic existence, and how all of those *do* make sense within the context of emptiness of intrinsic existence.

And Tsong-kha-pa (3: 132) continues:

> Therefore, those who currently claim to teach the meaning of Madhyamaka are actually giving the position of the essentialists when they hold that all causes and effects—such as the agents and the objects of production—are impossible in the absence of intrinsic existence. Thus, Nagarjuna the Protector holds that one must seek the emptiness of intrinsic existence and the middle way on the very basis of the teachings of cause and effect—that is, the production and cessation of specific effects in dependence upon specific causes and conditions. The twenty-fourth chapter of Nagarjuna's *Fundamental Wisdom* says, "That which arises dependently we explain as emptiness."

The twenty-fourth chapter of the *Fundamental Wisdom* illustrates a point we discussed earlier—that a more fully developed understanding of conventional and ultimate truth gives you the basis for a deeper comprehension of the four noble truths. Tsong-kha-pa (3: 135) says:

> This being the case, dependent arising is tenable within emptiness of intrinsic existence, and when dependent arising is tenable, suffering is also tenable—for suffering may be attributed only to what arises in dependence on causes and conditions . . .

The phrase "this being the case" refers to understanding emptiness in terms of the absence of *intrinsic* existence rather than the absence of existence.

Tsong-kha-pa is making this connection: Once you can maintain an understanding of ultimate reality as emptiness of *intrinsic* existence, not negating too much or too little, then you can understand dependent origination. And when dependent origination works within emptiness, then the notion of suffering is sustainable because suffering is a dependently arisen phenomenon. When you can understand suffering as a dependent-arising, within emptiness, then you can understand its origins. Among the origins of suffering, the real root is ignorance regarding the ultimate nature of reality. So understanding emptiness allows you to understand the possibility of cessation and a path to that cessation. The true path and the cessation to which it leads together constitute the true Dharma among the three jewels. When you can see how the Dharma jewel works within emptiness, then you can also envision individuals who embody that Dharma—and such persons constitute the Sangha. And if there is a Sangha, then *perfection* within that Sangha, its consummation and epitome, is the Buddha.

CHAPTER FOURTEEN

Finding the Middle Way

Analysis Refutes Intrinsic Nature

As Tsong-kha-pa sees it, Madhyamaka analysis does *not* eradicate conventional existence. He writes (3: 156):

> A proper analysis of whether these phenomena—forms and such—exist, or are produced, in an objective sense is what we call "a line of reasoning that analyzes reality" or "a line of reasoning that analyzes the final status of being." Since we Madhyamikas do not assert that the production of forms and such can withstand analysis by such reasoning, our position avoids the fallacy that there are truly existent things.

This leads to the challenge, "If these things cannot withstand rational analysis, then how is it possible for something to exist when reason has refuted it?" To which Tsong-kha-pa (3: 156) replies, "You are mistakenly conflating the inability to withstand rational analysis with invalidation by reason."

This is an extremely important point. When we have something like "arising" and we subject it to critical analysis, asking whether things come into being from themselves or from others or in some other way, then already we are entering the domain of ultimate analysis. But the existence of things is not posited from the ultimate standpoint; all phenomena are posited on the conventional level. Arising and other things cannot withstand ultimate analysis. But the fact that they cannot withstand ultimate analysis does *not* mean that ultimate analysis invalidates them or negates them.

This is the very same point that Gung-tang makes in the passage we discussed above:

> In the context of the philosophical view of emptiness, we are searching for intrinsic nature, so when we do not find that intrinsic nature, this constitutes the negation of *intrinsic nature.*[181]

It is not the negation of arising or existence. Thus, negating intrinsic existence by employing ultimate analysis does not destroy the conventional existence of things.

Reliable Means of Knowledge

Furthermore, Tsong-kha-pa (3: 163-175) shows that conventional phenomena are not refuted through investigation of whether they are established by valid cognition, which is to say, by reliable means of knowledge. Does Nagarjuna accept valid cognition?

There are sutra passages that state that the eyes, the nose, and the ears are not reliable means of knowledge.[182] Tsong-kha-pa explains that such passages are not actually rejecting valid cognition in general. The sutra in effect asks: If these sensory perceptions were reliable means of knowledge, then why would we need the paths of the noble beings, the perspective of enlightenment? This context allows us to get at what the sutra really means. As Tsong-kha-pa explains, this passage does not reject valid cognition in general, but rejects the idea that sensory perceptions can give reliable knowledge of the ultimate nature of things. When it comes to the final nature of reality, what we can rely on is not ordinary sense perception but the distinctive perspective of noble beings—yogic direct perceivers of the emptiness of intrinsic existence.

Until we are enlightened, at the perceptual level things appear to have inherent existence, so there is going to be an element of deception. But even though there is a flaw in how things appear, these perceptions are not totally invalid. They are mistaken about how things exist, but they are not totally unreliable. In Nagarjuna's own writing we find reference to four different means of reliable knowledge: direct perception, inferential cognition, cognition based upon testimony, and cognition based upon analogy.[183] But all forms of valid cognition can be included within two types, direct perception and inferential cognition. Analogical knowledge and testimony-based knowledge arise in distinctive ways and have distinctive roles, but indirectly they are also forms of inferential cognition.

Tsong-kha-pa (3: 164) then raises a more serious qualm. Chandrakirti's commentary on Aryadeva's *Four Hundred* says:

> It is quite inconsistent to call sensory consciousness "perception" and also to consider it valid with regard to other things. As the world sees it, a valid cognition is simply a nondeceptive consciousness; however, the Bhagavan said that even consciousness, because it is a composite, has a false and deceptive quality and is like a magician's illusion. That which has a false and deceptive quality and is like a magician's illusion is not nondeceptive because it exists in one way and appears in another. It is not right to designate such as a valid cognition because it would then absurdly follow that all consciousnesses would be valid cognitions.

This would *seem* to be a general refutation of the position that visual consciousnesses and such are valid cognitions. Tsong-kha-pa (3: 165) writes, "Unlike the passage 'Eye, ear, and nose are not valid,' this passage has been a source of grave doubt. Therefore, I will explain it in great detail." He (3: 165) goes on to explain:

> Chandrakirti does not accept even conventionally that anything exists essentially or by way of its intrinsic character. Thus, how could he accept this claim that the sensory

> consciousnesses are valid with regard to the intrinsic character of their objects? Therefore, this refutation of the claim that sensory consciousnesses are valid is a refutation of the view that they are valid with regard to the intrinsic character of the five objects.

When we talk about a certain perception or perspective as erroneous or invalid or deceptive, we have to know in relation to *what*? For example, in conceptual thought—even conceptual realization of emptiness—there is an element of distortion and error at the level of appearance. However, such minds can still be valid and reliable in regard to the objects that they comprehend. You have to distinguish the ways that objects appear from what is being apprehended and comprehended by the mind.

Chandrakirti is negating not valid cognition in general, but the particular notion of valid cognition held by other masters, including Bhavaviveka. For them, to say that sensory perceptions such as visual or auditory experiences are valid in relation to their objects means that they are valid in relation to the *intrinsic nature* of these objects. Chandrakirti is pointing out that sense perceptions are deceived or mistaken about the intrinsic character of their objects because they perceive objects as having an objective, inherent existence. The content of that perception—the object's inherent existence—is untenable because if things had such existence, then when critical analysis sought out this intrinsic nature it would become clearer and clearer, ever more obvious. Nagarjuna's *Precious Garland* gives this analogy: If a mirage were truly water, then the closer you got to it, the more obvious the water would become. Instead, as you approach the perception of water gradually dissolves.[184]

Chandrakirti points out that even our sensory perceptions are mistaken when it comes to the intrinsic nature of their objects because those objects lack the intrinsic nature that our senses perceive. Chandrakirti wants us to recognize the disparity between how we *perceive* things and how things really are. This disparity brings an element of distortion, a kind of invalidity, into even our ordinary perception.

And when we perceive things as having intrinsic nature, then we tend to assume that they actually do possess this objective and inherent existence. The perception of intrinsic reality becomes the basis for belief in inherent existence. For example, the Chittamatra school holds that things arise from other things that are intrinsically different. They say, "We don't need to establish the validity of the notion that things arise from other things because arising from other factors is something that we can directly perceive." They *perceive* things as intrinsically other and they use this misperception as a reason to support their belief in intrinsic existence.

Tsong-kha-pa (3: 165-166) continues:

> This refutation is made by way of the Bhagavan's [i.e., the Buddha's] statement that consciousness is false and deceptive. The statement that it is deceptive refutes its being nondeceptive, and this in turn refutes its validity because "that which is nondeceptive" is the definition of "valid cognition." In what sense is it deceptive? As Chandrakirti puts it, "it exists in one way but appears in another."

This is the disparity to which I referred. Tsong-kha-pa (3: 166) then writes:

> This means that the five objects—forms, sounds, and so forth—are not established by way of their intrinsic character, but appear to the sensory consciousnesses as though they were. Therefore, those sensory consciousnesses are not valid with regard to the intrinsic character of their objects. In brief, what Chandrakirti intended in this passage is that the sensory consciousnesses are not valid with regard to the intrinsic character of the five objects because they are deceived in relation to the appearance of the intrinsic character in the five objects. This is because those five objects are empty of

intrinsic character yet appear to have it. For example, it is like a consciousness that perceives two moons.

Tsong-kha-pa concludes (3: 166-167) that Chandrakirti's statement is refuting the position that sensory perceptions can be valid with respect to the intrinsic character of their objects; he is *not* negating the notion that the perceptions are valid in general. There certainly can be reliable knowledge of conventional objects.

Svatantrika and Intrinsic Existence

Among Madhyamikas, there are two camps: the Svatantrika accepts the notion of intrinsic nature—existence by way of essentially real characteristics—on the conventional level; the Prasangika rejects that notion even on the conventional level.

On what basis can we infer that Bhavaviveka and other followers of Svatantrika actually subscribe to the notion of intrinsic existence, existence by way of essentially real characteristics? One source is a passage in Bhavaviveka's *Blaze of Reasons*, an autocommentary on his *Heart of the Middle Way*: "In our case we accept the mental consciousnesses to be the actual referent of the term 'person.'"[185] This implies that he accepts that there is an identity of persons that can be found when you search for the ultimate referent of the term "person."

A second instance is found in Bhavaviveka's commentary on Nagarjuna's *Fundamental Wisdom*, wherein Bhavaviveka refutes the Chittamatra approach to interpreting sutra. In Chittamatra, the first turning of the wheel of Dharma is not definitive. The second turning does have definitive content—emptiness—but should not be read literally because the Perfection of Wisdom sutras negate intrinsic existence across the board, for all phenomena from visible forms up through the omniscient mind of a buddha. Chittamatra argues that this needs to be interpreted on the basis of the *Sutra Unravelling the Intended Meaning* from the third turning of the wheel.

According to Chittamatra, we need to read the negations of the

Perfection of Wisdom sutras contextually, identifying how they apply to different natures of phenomena. They speak of three natures: the imputed nature, the dependent nature, and the consummate nature. When the Buddha states in the Perfection of Wisdom sutras that "all phenomena lack intrinsic existence," this lack means different things in relation to each of the three natures. In relation to the dependent nature, intrinsic arising or ultimate arising is negated; for imputed phenomena, intrinsic existence or existence by way of essentially real characteristics is negated.

Tsong-kha-pa (3: 168-169) points out that, in criticizing the proponent of Chittamatra, Bhavaviveka's argument amounts to this: "You say that imputed phenomena are devoid of existence by way of real characteristics. So when you speak of 'imputed phenomena,' we can analyze that in terms of 'that which imputes' and 'that which is imputed.' When you reject the intrinsic existence of 'that which imputes,' then you reject the intrinsic existence of language and concepts because it is language and concepts that impute characteristics. If you say that language and concepts lack inherent existence, then you fall into the extreme of nihilism." By framing his criticism in this way, Bhavaviveka shows that he himself actually accepts the inherent existence of language, concepts, and so forth.

Likewise, when the Svatantrika scholar Kamalashila comments on the *Sutra Unravelling the Intended Meaning*, he qualifies all of the negations with phrases such as "within the ultimate," "from the ultimate point of view," or "on the ultimate level." Kamalashila also says that the *Sutra Unravelling the Intended Meaning* establishes the definitive reading of the scriptures. This means that Kamalashila accepts *that* sutra as itself being a definitive sutra. This shows that Kamalashila and his teacher Shantarakshita both subscribe to the notion that intrinsic nature does exist at the conventional level. Tsong-kha-pa (3: 170-172) also analyzes Bhavaviveka's Svatantrika position on the atomic structure of material things, teasing out the fact that Bhavaviveka's position implies an acceptance of intrinsic nature.

These sections of the *Great Treatise* are very difficult, quite tough.

There is a saying that when reading the more difficult sections of this text, you should be like a toothless old man trying to eat—what you cannot chew, you just swallow. For me, these sections are very difficult, so for you perhaps they are more difficult. For now, we will pass over these sections. When we come to this sort of thing, sometimes it's better for both the teacher and the student to take a little time off!

Conventional Knowledge

If our usual perceptions of everyday objects are mistaken about intrinsic nature, then why are they said to be conventionally true? To address this, Tsong-kha-pa (3: 173-174) explains that when we speak of conventional truth, the word "truth" does not connote objectivity but rather truth from the perspective of a particular mind. That conventional truths are called "truths" does not imply any acceptance of an objectively real nature in them.

Tsong-kha-pa (3: 177) goes on to explain that if we fail to identify the object of negation accurately, we may falsely think that the analysis that negates intrinsic nature even on the conventional level also undermines the validity of everyday transactions and conventions. This mistake can lead to a position where no distinction can be made between what is correct and what is incorrect in any context. Depending on what you take "true" to mean, the correct and the incorrect will either both be false or both be true—because neither has any intrinsic nature at all. This is a terrible mistake, of which Tsong-kha-pa (3: 178) writes:

> As a result, prolonged habituation to such a view does not bring you the least bit closer to the correct view. In fact, it takes you further away from it, for such a wrong view stands in stark contradiction to the path of dependent arising, the path in which all of the teachings on the dependent arising of cyclic existence and nirvana are tenable within our system.

Our perception of phenomena as possessing intrinsic nature is not correct because in fact none of them have any objective nature of their own. How, then, do we adjudicate what is correct and what is incorrect? Does emptiness mean that anything we think of becomes real? If we conjure in our imagination horns on a rabbit's head, we somehow have to be able to say that this does not actually make rabbit horns into something real.

Consider the case of a person who sees a coiled rope at twilight and mistakenly thinks it is a snake. We have to be able to say that the perception of the coiled rope as a snake is false. But there is also the case of perceiving a snake based upon the body of an actual snake. Without reference to intrinsic or objective nature, how do we adjudicate these two perceptions as wrong and right, respectively? No snake exists intrinsically in the coiled rope; no snake exists intrinsically in the body of the actual snake. So in this regard they are exactly the same, yet one perception is right and the other wrong. We accord only nominal existence, conventional existence, to things—but that does not mean that anything goes. It does not mean that whatever we imagine is just as real as anything can be.

Tsong-kha-pa (3: 178) explains conventional existence this way:

> How does one determine whether something exists conventionally? We hold that something exists conventionally (1) if it is known to a conventional consciousness; (2) if no other conventional valid cognition contradicts its being as it is thus known; and (3) if reason that accurately analyzes reality—that is, analyzes whether something intrinsically exists—does not contradict it. We hold that what fails to meet those criteria does not exist.

These are the criteria by which one can distinguish a perception that is false from a perception that is correct. Nothing has any inherent nature, but at the level of everyday experience there are still harms and benefits, right and wrong. These distinctions do not depend on things having intrinsic reality.

Two Types of Madhyamaka

When Madhyamikas pose their arguments, there is a question about whether it is appropriate to use autonomous syllogisms (*svatantra*).[186] Tsong-kha-pa (3: 254-255) explains that when we try to understand what is really at issue here, it is helpful to understand the two standpoints as representing one group that subscribes to the notion of intrinsic existence and another that rejects intrinsic existence even on a conventional level. Speaking of proponents and opponents of intrinsic nature is actually clearer than the terms Svatantrika and Prasangika. Masters such as Buddhapalita mainly use arguments that draw out consequences (*prasanga*), revealing internal contradiction in the others' position. In contrast, Bhavaviveka and Shantarakshita use—and argue that one *should* use—primarily syllogistic reasoning rather than contradictory consequences. Tsong-kha-pa argues that the position of Bhavaviveka and Shantarakshita is grounded in the tacit assumption that things have intrinsic nature.

Is it indispensable to use syllogistic reasoning in order to generate inferential understanding? Or can reasoning in the form of a contradictory consequence also generate inference? This is one aspect of the debate. The usual assumption is that when two parties enter into dialectical analysis, the subject of the discourse must be commonly verified. It should be something that is mutually accepted, without the imposition of either party's distinctive philosophical or metaphysical view about how it exists. The subject has to be accepted at a level where both parties share a notion of its existence. Chandrakirti criticizes Bhavaviveka's basic assumption that this is even possible when Madhyamikas debate with non-Madhyamikas about emptiness.

Tsong-kha-pa gives two slightly different explanations of the crucial passages on this from Chandrakirti's *Clear Words*; one is here in the *Great Treatise on the Stages of the Path to Enlightenment* and the other is in his *Essence of Eloquence.* Here, Tsong-kha-pa gives the following reading. When a Samkhya[187] philosopher says that a sprout arises in some ultimate sense, then Bhavaviveka would refute them by posing a syllogism directly asserting that a sprout does *not* ultimately arise. Chandrakirti points out that when Bhavaviveka does this, he is assuming the Madhyamika and the Samkhya have a commonly appearing subject, the sprout, about which they can debate in this way. However, for the Madhyamika, the sprout is posited only conventionally; it does not hold up under ultimate analysis and thus the conventional mind that takes the sprout as real is a form of a distorted cognition. It does not perceive the sprout as it actually exists. The Samkhya philosopher, on the other hand, believes that the sprout is verified by a valid cognition that gives a true picture of the sprout's intrinsic nature. So when Samkhyas and Madhyamikas enter into a discussion pertaining to the ultimate status of a sprout, there will be no commonly established understanding of the subject. Without this, how can you insist on using syllogistic reasoning in a way that presupposes such a commonly appearing subject? Tsong-kha-pa sees Chandrakirti as pointing out this contradiction in Bhavaviveka's position.

In *Essence of Eloquence*, Tsong-kha-pa reads this passage in Chandrakirti's *Clear Words* in a slightly different way.[188] Again, however, the main point is that when a proponent of intrinsic nature and the proponent of a standpoint that rejects intrinsic existence enter into a debate, there cannot be a commonly verified subject. This is because the proponent of intrinsic existence assumes that the subject of the debate is verified by valid cognition that is nondeceptive about the subject's having intrinsic nature. The Madhyamika, on the other hand, assumes that the subject being examined has no intrinsic nature, so any perception that relates to it as if it possessed intrinsic nature is going to be distorted. Therefore, there are no commonly accepted criteria for validating the subject that is being analyzed.

The main point of contention really is whether one accepts the notion of inherent existence or intrinsic nature. When an ordinary valid cognition, a reliable conventional mind, perceives an object, is it or is it not mistaken about its object having intrinsic nature? Things *appear* to have intrinsic existence, but do they actually have it or not?

Chandrakirti's *Commentary on the Middle Way*, before specifically refuting the Chittamatra standpoint, critiques another perspective that rejects true existence but still accords intrinsic existence to things conventionally.[189] While the term "Svatantrika" is not used here, this is a critique of the Svatantrika position. It is a position that acknowledges that all things are empty of true existence, they are empty of ultimate existence, but still claims that since they do exist conventionally, they must be able to exist by way of their own distinctive characteristics.

Against this view Chandrakirti points out three contradictory consequences. First, he says that if this view were correct, then the wisdom of the meditative equipoise of enlightened beings would cause the destruction of things and events because in fact they recognize all of these as utterly devoid of inherent existence. Second, he says that if this view were correct, then conventional truths would withstand ultimate analysis. If we search for the very essence of the person, analyzing its ultimate nature, and then identify its essential characteristic as the *mental consciousness*, then the person actually is something that can withstand ultimate analysis. This contradicts the Madhyamaka idea that everything is empty of ultimate existence because nothing can withstand such analysis. Third, he argues that if this view were correct, then the teaching that all conditioned phenomena are devoid of ultimate arising would not hold up because ultimate arising remains and is still not refuted. Chandrakirti goes on to say that the position that he is critiquing also contradicts the *Questions of Upali Sutra*, where emptiness is presented as the emptiness of intrinsic existence, emptiness of own-being.

When we speak of things as self-empty, empty of their own essential or intrinsic nature, we have to be careful and clear. If you just assume that a form, in order to exist and be a form, must have some essential nature, then when you hear that this form is empty you might think that emptiness is a negation of some additional, ultimate reality that is lacking in the form. The problem with understanding emptiness in this way is that it leaves forms as we now perceive them intact. You are trying to negate something over and above that. It is to address this that the Perfection of Wisdom sutras teach that it is not the case that visible forms and other phenomena are emptied of something extra by emptiness; rather form itself is emptiness. If we think that the form is intrinsically real, but emptiness negates its having some ultimate nature beyond that, then we have not really understood emptiness. We have to take the form as we perceive it and then negate its inherent existence. This kind of self-emptiness is what the *Questions of Upali Sutra* teaches and this is what Tsong-kha-pa accepts.

In what is called the Great Madhaymaka system of Tibet there is a quite different sense of the term "self-empty," according to which all conventional realities are self-empty, empty of their own essential natures, while the ultimate truth is empty of other things. According to this view, the ultimate truth is understood to be ultimately real, absolute.[190]

How to Proceed

If rejecting intrinsic existence means rejecting autonomous syllogistic reasoning—because there is no commonly appearing subject—then does that mean that Prasangikas accept no forms of reasoning at all? Tsong-kha-pa (3: 267-275) says that this is not the case. One can employ different forms of argumentation, including consequential reasoning that takes into account the perspective of the other person. As we have seen, when you are trying to establish emptiness for someone who assumes that things have inherent existence, the debate begins with no commonly verified subject. Nonetheless, the Prasangika can take into account the perspective of the other person and on that basis simply analyze the subject as it is known to that opponent. As Tsong-kha-pa (3: 274) says in concluding this section:

> So, when the reason that is used to prove the *probandum* is established for both parties with the kind of valid cognition

> explained previously, this is an autonomous (*svatantra*) reason. When the reason is not established in that way and the *probandum* is proven using the three criteria that the *other* party, the opponent, accepts as being present, this constitutes the Prasangika method. It is quite clear that this is what the master Chandrakirti intended.

Which system should we follow? Tsong-kha-pa writes:

> The great Madhyamikas who follow the noble father Nagarjuna and his spiritual son Aryadeva split into two different systems: Prasangika and Svatantrika. Which do we follow? Here, we are followers of the Prasangika system. Moreover, as explained previously, we refute essential or intrinsic nature even conventionally; yet all that has been taught about cyclic existence and nirvana must be fully compatible with that refutation.

Having stated that we should follow the Prasangika system in establishing the view of emptiness, Tsong-kha-pa then explains how to develop the correct view of emptiness on that basis. He describes how to realize the selflessness of person, the selflessness of phenomena, and how to clear away obscurations through familiarization with that view.

You realize the emptiness of the person on the basis of an analogy with the analysis of a chariot. A chariot is a composite entity, dependent on its parts; when subjected to sevenfold analysis it is proven to be unfindable. With the same sevenfold reasoning, you can analyze the person, investigating its relationship to the mental and physical aggregates. In this way, you come to know that the person is empty of inherent existence. You can then extend that analysis to the "mine," the things that belong to that person. Both "I" and "mine" are empty.

You can then refute the notion of a self of phenomena by analyzing how things might arise in four possible ways—from self, other, both, or neither. It was precisely in this analysis of whether things can arise from themselves that Buddhapalita's commentary on Nagarjuna's *Fundamental Wisdom* was subject to extensive criticism by Bhavaviveka, in response to which Chandrakirti demonstrated that Bhavaviveka's objections do not really hold up. This is where there arose the whole discussion on whether there is a commonly verified subject when Madhyamikas debate with non-Madhyamikas about emptiness.

How, then, does meditating on emptiness clear away obscurations? Tsong-kha-pa (3: 320) writes:

> After you have seen that the self and that which belongs to that self lack even the slightest particle of intrinsic nature, you can accustom yourself to these facts, thereby stopping the reifying view of the perishing aggregates as the self and that which belongs to the self. When you stop that view, you will stop the four types of grasping—grasping that holds on to what you want, etc.—explained earlier. When you stop these, existence conditioned by attachment will not occur; hence, there will be an end to the rebirth of the aggregates conditioned by existence; you will attain liberation. Nagarjuna's *Fundamental Wisdom* says:
>
> > Because of the pacification of the self and that which the self owns,
> > The conception "I" and the conception "mine" will be gone.[191]

Tsong-kha-pa (3: 321) then really sums up the importance of understanding emptiness:

> Thus, afflictions such as attachment and hostility—rooted in the reifying view of the perishing aggregates—are produced from such misconceptions. These misconceptions operate mistakenly only by clinging to the notion "This is real" in regard to the eight worldly concerns,[192] or men and women,

> or pot, cloth, form, or feeling. Since it is these misconceptions that conceive those objects, they are generated from the elaboration of conceptions of true existence.

After citing passages from Chandrakirti that establish this point, Tsong-kha-pa (3: 322) concludes:

> [T]he view of emptiness cuts the root of cyclic existence and is the heart of the path to liberation. Hence, you must gain firm certainty about this.

You may not be interested in seeking liberation. You may not even be wondering about it. But if you *do* aspire to liberation, then you have to cultivate an understanding of emptiness.

Meditation on Emptiness

When you negate inherent existence, there is nothing at all left as an objective ground or basis for existence. Tsong-kha-pa (3: 325) emphasizes just how hard it is to posit the dependent origination of cause and effect within a world devoid of inherent existence. Yet, you still need to maintain the functions of harm and benefit, cause and effect, and so on. In the aftermath of a thorough-going negation of objective reality, how can we have any coherent notion of reality at all? We have to accept that reality is merely nominal, merely conventional. Tsong-kha-pa makes this same point in his *Ocean of Reasoning* and his *Illumination of the Thought.* He says that it is comparatively easy to understand emptiness by means of negation; the great difficulty and challenge in Madhyamaka philosophy is how, in the wake of that negation, to understand reality in terms of dependent origination.

Here it is most helpful to remember Tsong-kha-pa's three criteria for conventional existence. In order to be conventionally existent something must be known to worldly convention, but it also must not be invalidated by any other valid conventional cognition. This other cognition might be your own subsequent cognitions. You might at first perceive something and think that it is as it appears, but then yourself later see that this is in fact not the case. Or your initial perception could be invalidated by valid cognitions of some other person. We can compare this to the idea of verification in the scientific method, where an important principle is repeatability and intersubjective verification, verification by some other person.

The third criterion for conventional existence is not being invalidated by ultimate analysis. This criterion provides a way to make judgments about metaphysical claims. For example, some followers of the Mind-Only School posit a foundational consciousness (*alaya*). They may not see themselves as having made this postulation from the point of view of ultimate analysis. However, from the Prasangika Madhyamaka perspective, postulating a foundational consciousness as the true essence of the person is a mistaken form of ultimate analysis because this claim is made in the context of not being satisfied with everyday conventions. Determined to find a real and objectively grounded referent of the term "person," they put forward the foundational consciousness. Proponents of a foundational consciousness are uncomfortable with the idea of just saying that the mental consciousness is the person; they want something much more stable. But the claim that a foundational consciousness is the real basis of the person is invalidated by ultimate analysis.

In actual meditative practice you must use and become very familiar with reasonings such as the sevenfold analysis of person or the fourfold analysis of whether a phenomenon is produced from itself, another, both, or neither. As you apply reasoning, rejecting one possibility after another, you finally come to recognize that the subject under analysis cannot be found when searched for in this way. You get a sense that the thing you are analyzing does not exist under investigation and cannot at all hold up in the face of such scrutiny.

At this point it is crucial to remember that *things do exist.* This is incontrovertible because things do have effects, they do make an impact. They can cause harm; they can bring benefit. So they definitely exist in some way. And you will then begin to understand what it means to accord things status as nominally existent.

Next, after doing this analytical negation, it is most helpful to reconnect your meditation on emptiness to the principle of dependent origination. Meditate further on emptiness, but now use dependent origination as the reason to show that things are empty. The fact that things are dependently originated demonstrates their lack of any independent status. Being dependent, they are thoroughly contingent; their nature is such that they cannot be real in themselves, but exist only in relation. You then see that the only existence we can accord to things is relational. The existence of things is comprehensible and possible only in terms of dependent designation.

Buddhapalita says that if things existed in their own right, by means of their own intrinsic nature, then we ought to be able to point our finger at it and say, "That is the essence!" And in that case there would be no need for the thing to depend on any other factors or conditions. Also, Nagarjuna's *Pulverizing the Categories* argues that if things had objective reality, some way of existing by means of their own essence or intrinsic nature, then the thought, "this is so" should arise even before they are designated or labeled.[193] In fact, the thought that something is such-and-such, an identity-based thought, can arise only when something is dependently designated. If things had their own essential natures, then recognizing them as such should not depend upon their being labeled. Reflecting on this is a way to recognize that the only reality that we can accord to things is nominal, dependent reality.

If you get some understanding of this, then you should cultivate your understanding further and further. Then compare your understanding to the way that things usually appear. Through contemplating emptiness you have come to recognize that things and events do not possess existence by means of intrinsic nature; they have no inherent existence. Yet in your own everyday perception of the world you still tend to perceive things as possessing such objective existence. Noticing this, you come to a powerful recognition of the deep disparity between the way things appear to you and the way things really are. This brings experiential flavor into the process of identifying the object of negation. When you turn your mind again to identifying the object of negation, your own sense of how things exist objectively, it seems almost as if you are touching something in a naked way.

So, in actual practice, we need to combine and work back and forth between various approaches. First, use critical reasoning to demonstrate that anything you examine is, at last, untenable under analysis. Then, reflect on dependent origination, the merely relational existence of these unfindable things. After that, compare the understanding you develop in this way to your own personal everyday perception of the world. This brings to life your sense of what we are doing as we grasp at things as objectively real.

In this way you will come to see how understanding dependent origination leads to emptiness and how understanding of emptiness leads to dependent origination. You will see how these understandings complement and reinforce another. As Tsong-kha-pa says in his *Three Principal Aspects of the Path:*[194]

> When these two understandings do not alternate but are
> simultaneous
> So that just seeing unfailing dependent arising
> Is the knowledge that destroys all grasping at objects,
> You have reached the culmination of the analysis of the view.

Tsong-kha-pa (3: 327-330) then concludes the *Great Treatise* by explaining the various types of analytical insight. He describes (3: 330-359) how to cultivate and maintain insight and how to unite serenity and insight. He concludes (3: 361-365) with a summary of the entire path and a brief description of how to train in Vajrayana.

CHAPTER FIFTEEN

Toward Buddhahood

So now we are done. To understand this teaching properly takes months. After that, to practice it properly takes many decades. But we have to do it. There is no other choice. In my own case, I developed a genuine interest in these teachings when I was about sixteen years old; now I am seventy-three. All along, this has been my main guidebook.

In Tibetan we call texts that are very comprehensive "a thousand doses at once." Tsong-kha-pa's *Great Treatise on the Stages of the Path to Enlightenment* is such a text. But Tsong-kha-pa is unique in that he sets out to explain the hardest passages in the Indian texts.[195] Naturally, this makes his own books very difficult, but clarifying the difficult passages is necessary and worthwhile. His collected works fill eighteen volumes in Tibetan; there are writings of every sort, but hardly any of it is easy reading. Every text says something weighty, something of profound significance. At the same time, his writing style is wonderful; he uses just a few words to express the greatest meaning. It is a special gift to be able to write in this way.

As a simple Buddhist monk I am extremely happy to lecture on this book. Of course my own knowledge is still very limited and my experience even more limited. But reading this book makes me feel very happy and fortunate.

Look at your teacher. From age sixteen until now at age seventy-three I have been working on it and I am still working on it. For you also, the study and practice of these teachings will take many, many years. Do not feel discouraged or demoralized. Each day, every day, learn one page. That's enough. That is good. Then, after one hundred days, you will know one hundred pages; after one thousand days, you will know one thousand pages.

Even the construction of external things takes time, so building something in our minds takes time and is not easy. But I have total certainty that our minds *can* change and improve. I assure you of this much from my own experience. If you make effort continuously, without losing interest, without losing determination, things will change. Things will improve.

Eventually our aim is genuine experience of infinite altruism and perfect understanding of ultimate reality. As Buddhists our final destination is buddhahood. However far it may be, let us start right now for that final destination.

Thank you.

Dedication

As is customary during the stages of the path teachings, today we conclude by chanting together the aspiration portion of Tsong-kha-pa's dedicatory verses in the *Great Treatise* (3: 368-369):

By accumulating through long effort
The two collections as vast as the sky
May I become the chief of the conquerors,
Guide of all beings whose minds are blinded by ignorance.

Also, in all lives until I reach that point
May Mañjughosha look after me with loving-kindness.
After I find the supreme path, complete in the stages of the teaching,
By accomplishing it may I please the conquerors.

By skill in means inspired by strong loving-kindness,
May the vital points of the path that I precisely know

Clear away the mental darkness of beings.
May I then uphold the Conqueror's teachings for a long time.

In regions where the supreme, precious teaching has not spread
Or where it has spread but then declined,
May I illumine that treasure of happiness and benefit
With a mind deeply moved by great compassion.

May this treatise on the stages of the path to enlightenment,
Well-founded on the wondrous deeds of the conquerors and their children,
Bring glory to the minds of those who want to be free,
And long preserve the Conqueror's achievements.

As for all who provide conditions that support integration of the good path
And clear away conditions that inhibit that integration,
Whether they are human or not, may they never be separated in all their lifetimes
From the pure path praised by the conquerors.

When I strive to properly achieve the supreme vehicle
Through the ten deeds of the teaching,
May I be accompanied always by those who have power
And may an ocean of good fortune pervade all directions.

Long Life Prayer

Joshua Cutler: Thank you, Your Holiness, for your wonderful teachings. Our teacher, our founder, Geshe Wangyal, always referred to Your Holiness as a "wish-granting jewel." Every time I meet Your Holiness, I feel the force of those words; I sense that my wishes are being fulfilled. In just six days of teachings you have given us the heart of the *Great Treatise*. Only a great scholar of the Dharma could do that.

I would like everyone here to join me in reciting, three times, this verse for His Holiness's long life:

In that pure land surrounded by snowy mountains
You are the source of all benefit and happiness,
All powerful Avalokiteshvara, Tenzin Gyatso,
May you stay until samsara's end.

Notes

1 See *The Great Treatise on the Stages of the Path to Enlightenment*, 3 vols. (Ithaca, N.Y.: Snow Lion Publications, 2001, 2002, and 2004), hereafter usually referred to as *Great Treatise.*

2 The event was hosted, in close partnership with Lehigh University, by the Tibetan Buddhist Learning Center of Washington, New Jersey. This center was founded by the Mongolian scholar Geshe Ngawang Wangyal (1901-1983), who was the first Buddhist teacher of several prominent Buddhists in the West, including Jeffrey Hopkins and Robert Thurman. See www.labsum.org.

3 Tsong-kha-pa Losang Drakpa (1357-1419) founded the Geluk order of Tibetan Buddhism, of which the Dalai Lama is a member. Located in northern Bihar (India), Nalanda flourished as one of world's great libraries and universities between the fifth and twelfth centuries. His Holiness often argues that Tibet has uniquely inherited from Nalanda the full richness of Indian Buddhist scholarship. See his "Praise to Seventeen Nalanda Masters" in his *The Middle Way* (Boston: Wisdom Publications, 2009), 153-161.

4 His Holiness's riveting memoir, *My Land and My People* (New York: McGraw-Hill, 1962), relates how Chinese threats and provocations led to his decision to leave Tibet and how he fled Chinese-occupied Lhasa. Norbulingka was the Dalai Lama's summer residence, shelled by the Chinese shortly after the Dalai Lama's escape.

5 The theme of global responsibility has been a constant in His Holiness's teachings. Particularly notable treatments of this theme are found in his *A Human Approach to World Peace* (Boston: Wisdom Publications, 1984) and his *Ethics for the New Millenium* (New York: Riverhead Books, 2001).

6 See note 3 above on Nalanda.

7 On the morning of Wednesday, July 9, 2008, the Dalai Lama visited the Dargah Sharif tomb-shrine in Ajmer, Rajasthan (India) to offer prayers on the occasion of "Urs," the death anniversary (796th) of a great Sufi, Kwaja Moinuddin Chishti. An estimated one million devotees from India, Bangladesh, Pakistan, and elsewhere visited the shrine during the six-day event.

8 Following the model of Muhammad, Muslim men throughout the world cover their heads, at least during prayer. *Tagiyah* is the general Arabic word for such caps; in Pakistan and India they are called *topi.*

9 Jamma Masjid, in Delhi, is one of the largest mosques in India. Mughal emperor Shah Jahan built it in 1658.

10 For example, Nalanda University—often cited by His Holiness as the main source of Tibetan Buddhism—was apparently razed by Bhaktiya Khalji in 1193. According to the received story, he first asked if there was a copy of the *Qur'an* in the library before destroying it.

11 The Mahabodhi Temple at Bodhgaya is regarded as the site of the Buddha's enlightenment; it is a UNESCO World Heritage site. It was built in the fifth or sixth century A.D. on the site of an earlier temple built by Ashoka (third century B.C.). While subject to raids, substantial damage, and neglect between the twelfth and nineteenth centuries, it was not destroyed and has been partially restored. Bodhgaya is located in Bihar, India, where about 14% of the population is Muslim. The major mosque in Bodhgaya is just southeast of the Mahabodhi temple compound.

12 A series of civil disturbances in Tibet began on March 10, 2008, the forty-ninth anniversary of the failed uprising of 1959 against Beijing's rule. Protests against the imprisonment of monks eventually became violent and included Tibetans attacking Han Chinese in Lhasa. Wen Jiabao, Premier of the People's Republic of China, accused the Dalai Lama of masterminding the violence. The Dalai Lama denied the accusation and said that the uprisings were caused by widespread discontent in Tibet.

13 His Holiness uses the phrase "Sanskrit tradition" to refer to Mahayana Buddhism insofar as Mahayana relies on scriptures originally written in the Sanskrit language. Since "Sanskrit" here signifies Mahayana, His Holiness is able to say below that the Chinese language is most important for the study of the Sanskrit Buddhist tradition. In contradistinction, His Holiness's phrase "the Pali tradition" refers to practices based on Buddhist scriptures preserved in Pali, the language of the (non-Mahayana) Theravada Buddhist scriptures.

14 Theosophy is a religious philosophy initially taught by Helena Blavatsky (1831-1891). The Theosophical Society was founded in 1875 in New York City, but in 1882 moved its headquarters to Adyar, near Chennai (= Madras), India.

15 This hesitancy is an expression of His Holiness' reluctance to promote Buddhism as a religion among those of a different heritage.

16 In reference to the prolific Geluk scholar Gung-tang Gonchog Denbay Dronmay (1763-1823). His writings are used extensively at the Go-mang College of Drebung Monastery and include popular collections of practical advice. Cited here and below is verse 2 from his "Verses of Advice on How to Meditate on Impermance." See Blanche C. Olschak and Geshe Thupten Wangyal's translation *Spiritual Guide to the Jewel Island* (Zürich: Buddhist Publications, 1973), 98-99.

17 As His Holiness states above (page 1), there is no question that Tsong-kha-pa is the author of the *Great Treatise on the Stages of the Path to Enlightenment*. His Holiness's statement that Atisha is the author alludes to an unusual passage within Tsong-kha-pa's *Great Treatise* (1: 34-35): "In particular, the text for this work is Atisha's *Lamp for the Path to Enlightenment*; hence, the very author of the *Lamp for the Path to Enlightenment* is also the author of this [book]." This has been the subject of much comment; it is not typical or traditional for someone authoring a book to state that the author of that very book is someone else. His Holiness gives one common interpretation below.

18 Atisha, and thus Tsong-kha-pa, differentiates beings of three capacities: small,

medium, and great. The religious practitioners among the small are beings whose aim is to have a good rebirth in the future; the medium are those who seek liberation from cyclic existence for themselves; the great are those who seek buddhahood for the welfare of all. Atisha organizes Buddhist practices according to how they are appropriate to persons of these capacities, thus showing how all the teachings are important along the path. See the discussion below in chapter 7. See also Geshe Sonam Rinchen and Ruth Sonam's *Atisha's Lamp for the Path* (Ithaca, N.Y.: Snow Lion Publications, 1997).

19 Manjushri is the bodhisattva who embodies the wisdom of the buddhas. See the discussion of enlightened bodhisattvas in the Dalai Lama's "Deities" in his *Kindness, Clarity, and Insight*, rev. ed. (Ithaca, N.Y.: Snow Lion Publications, 2006), 111-115.

20 See Geshe Wangyal's translation in *The Jewelled Staircase* (Ithaca, N.Y.: Snow Lion Publications, 1986), 50.

21 P5709, 83.4.6-7.

22 See Jeffrey Hopkins's translation, *Nagarjuna's Precious Garland* (Ithaca, N.Y.: Snow Lion Publications, 2007). His Holiness is most likely referring to verse 212: "A buddha's embodiment of form arises from the collection of merit; the embodiment of truth, O King, arises from the collection of wisdom." Elsewhere in the *Precious Garland*, Nagarjuna summarizes the causes of buddhahood in other (but not contradictory) ways: verses 174-175 call for the spirit of enlightenment, nondualistic wisdom, and compassion; verses 435-439 indicate that buddhahood is achieved through the six perfections (generosity, ethical discipline, patience, joyous perseverance, meditative stabilization, and wisdom) along with compassion.

23 The four noble truths are true sufferings, true origins, true cessations, and true paths. The first of these is our condition in cyclic existence, afflicted not only by physical pain and mental anguish but also by many subtler types of dissatisfaction. The second is the source of this condition, actions motivated by consciousnesses afflicted with greed, ill-will, and delusion. True cessations are dissolutions of suffering and its sources; this refers to the peace of nirvana. True paths are mental states that we can deliberately practice so as to attain true cessations.

24 The ultimate truth is the ultimate nature of all things as empty of intrinsic nature; conventional truths include all other existing things.

25 This topic is initially presented in chapter 5 and discussed in greater detail in chapter 7.

26 As can be seen in Gavin Kilty's translation, *The Splendor of an Autumn Moon* (Boston: Wisdom Publications, 2001), 216-245, or in Thupten Jinpa's translation at www.tibetanclassics.org/Jinpa_Translations.html. His Holiness's oral teachings on this text are available on the DVD *In Praise of Dependent Origination* (San Jose, Calif.: Gyuto Vajrayana Center, 2009).

27 As, for example, in Nagarjuna's *Sixty Stanzas*, translated by Geshe Thupten Jinpa at www.tibetanclassics.org/pdfs/SixtyStanzas.pdf.

28 Manjushri is the head of the profound lineage and Maitreya, of the vast lineage. This means that they are respectively the preeminent teachers of wisdom and compassionate action. Maitreya is also the bodhisattva who will become the next buddha of our world.

29 Vajrayana refers to the practice of tantric Buddhism. Vajrayana is based upon and necessitates general Mahayana practice deriving from Buddhist sutras. The Dalai Lama considers Vajrayana to be a form of Mahayana Buddhism, with the same goal (perfect enlightenment) and principles (wisdom and compassion) but with enhanced techniques, especially the technique of deity yoga, which involves envisioning oneself with real conviction as already being the fully enlightened being one is seeking to become.

30 Tsong-kha-pa cites this passage from Aryadeva's *Four Hundred* (8.15) at *Great Treatise* 1: 141. See Geshe Sonam Rinchen and Ruth Sonam's translation, *Aryadeva's Four Hundred Stanzas on the Middle Way* (Ithaca, N.Y.: Snow Lion Publications, 2008), 239.

31 This verse from Aryadeva's *Four Hundred* (12.1) is cited by Tsong-kha-pa at *Great Treatise* 1: 75.

32 Potowa Rinchen-sel (1027-1105) was one of the main students of Drom-don-pa (1004-1064), Drom-don-pa being one of Atisha's primary students and successors. For a broader picture of Potowa's crucial and highly creative role in spreading Atisha's form of Buddhism among the ordinary people of Tibet, see Ronald Davidson's *Tibetan Renaissance* (New York: Columbia University Press, 2005), 249-255.

33 For the *Jataka Tales*, see the translations by Chalmers and others in several volumes and editions and also readily available on-line. For the *Collection of Aphorisms*, see Gareth Sparham's translation as *The Tibetan Dhammapada* (London: Wisdom Publications, 1995).

34 Robert Thurman and associates have translated the *Ornament for the Mahayana Sutras* and published it as *The Universal Vehicle Discourse Literature* (New York: American Institute of Buddhist Studies, 2004).

35 Below (page 21), His Holiness gives an alternative explanation for these three sets of two texts. Cecil Bendall and W. H. D. Rouse's early twentieth-century translation of *Compendium of Instructions, Siksha-Samuccaya*, has been reissued (Whitefish, Mont.: Kessinger Publishing, 2008). *Engaging in the Bodhisattva Deeds* appears in several good English versions, including Kate Crosby and Andrew Skilton's *The Bodhicaryavatara* (Oxford: Oxford University Press, 1995).

36 The extensive writings of Gyel-tsap (1362-1432), one of Tsong-kha-pa's closest disciples, include *Heart Ornament of Explanation*—a long explanation of the *Ornament of Clear Realization*, a text which summarizes numerous categories and lists presented in the Perfection of Wisdom sutras. See the translation of the *Ornament of Clear Realization* along with commentary by Khenchen Thrangu Rinpoche in *The Ornament of Clear Realization* (Auckland, New Zealand: Zhyisil Chokyi Ghatsal, 2004); the commentary by itself was published in Khenchen Thrangu Rinpoche's *The Ornament of Clear Realization* (Delhi: Sri Satguru, 2001); and translation of the root text with Indian commentary and subcommentary in Gareth Sparham's *Abhisamayalamkara with Vrtti and Aloka*, 4 vols. (Fremont, Calif.: Jain Publishing Company, 2006-2011).

37 The traditional list of the eight texts: (1) *Great Treatise on the Stages of the Path* by Tsong-kha-pa, (2) *Medium Treatise on the Stages of the Path* by Tsong-kha-pa, and (3) *Concise Meaning of the Stages of the Path* by Tsong-kha-pa, (4) *Refined Gold of the Stages of the Path* by Sonam Gyatso (the Third Dalai Lama), (5) *Personal Instruc-*

tions from Manjushri by Ngawang Losang Gyatso (the Fifth Dalai Lama), (6) *Path to Bliss* by Losang Chokyi Nyima (the First Panchen Lama), (7) *Quick Path* by Losang Yeshe (the Second Panchen Lama), and (8) *Essence of Well-Spoken Advice* by Dagpo Khenchen Ngawang Drakpa. For more on these and on other related literature, see D. S. Ruegg's introduction to *Great Treatise* (1: 28-31).

38 See *Mind in Comfort and Ease* (Boston: Wisdom Publications, 2007) for the Dalai Lama's teachings on this text by the Nyingma master Long-chen-pa (1308-1364).

39 Translated by Geshe Wangyal and Brian Cutillo as *Illuminations* (Novato, Calif.: Lotsawa, 1988).

40 His Holiness does not here mention the fourth main sect of Tibetan Buddhism, Geluk; this is his own lineage, founded by Tsong-kha-pa, the author of the *Great Treatise on the Stages of the Path to Enlightenment.*

41 The reference here is to (1) turning away from attachment to this life, (2) turning away from attachment to future lives in cyclic existence, (3) turning away from attachment to nirvana for oneself alone, and (4) turning away from ignorance about the means of attaining buddhahood. See Gampopa's *Jewel Ornament of Liberation*, translated by Herbert Guenther (Boston: Shambhala, 1971), 41. On the characteristics of "stages of the path" (*lam rim*) literature and its relationship to other similar literature, see David Jackson's "The *bsTan rim* ('Stages of the Doctrine') and Similar Graded Expositions of the Bodhisattva Path" in José Cabezón and Roger Jackson, eds., *Tibetan Literature* (Ithaca, N.Y.: Snow Lion Publications, 1995), 229-243.

42 See Jeffrey Hopkins's translation, *Nagarjuna's Precious Garland* (Ithaca, N.Y.: Snow Lion Publications, 2007).

43 A reference to Vaibhashika, Sautrantika, Chittamatra, and Madhyamaka, a fourfold schema within which Tibetans classify Indian Buddhist philosophers. See Geshe Sopa and Jeffrey Hopkins's *Cutting Through Appearances* (Ithaca, N.Y.: Snow Lion Publication, 1989) and Guy Newland's *Appearance and Reality* (Ithaca, N.Y.: Snow Lion Publications, 1999).

44 Jonang refers to the tradition popularized by Shay-rap Gyal-tsen (1292-1361). See Cyrus Stearns's *The Buddha from Dölpo*, rev. and enl. ed. (Ithaca, N.Y.: Snow Lion Publications, 2010) and Jeffrey Hopkins's *Mountain Doctrine* (Ithaca, N.Y.: Snow Lion Publications, 2006), especially the excellent introduction. Part two of Jeffrey Hopkins's *Tsong-kha-pa's Final Exposition of Wisdom* (Ithaca, N.Y., Snow Lion Publications, 2008) compares the views of Shay-rap Gyal-tsen and Tsong-kha-pa in a helpful and evenhanded way.

45 Shugden is a controversial deity associated with the Dalai Lama's Geluk sect of Tibetan Buddhism. His Holiness's rejection of Shugden worship in 1975 was linked to his concern that worship of this deity promotes sectarian intolerance; he argues that Shugden is not—contrary to the claims of some others—an enlightened being. His Holiness also comments on this at: www.dalailama.com/page.123.htm. See also Georges Dreyfus's "The Shuk-den Affair" in *Journal of the International Association of Buddhist Studies* 21, no. 2 (1998): 227-270; this article also appears at www.dalailama.com/page.149.htm.

46 As seen in the Fifth Dalai Lama's *Collected Works*, vol. Ha, 423-4, as well as in the Fifth's autobiography. For context, see Dreyfus's article cited just above.

47 For a discussion of the relationship between Buddhism and science, see His Holiness's *The Universe in a Single Atom* (New York: Morgan Road Books, 2005).

48 There are a great many translations and studies of the *Heart Sutra* available in English, including the Dalai Lama's own *Essence of the Heart Sutra* (Boston: Wisdom Publications, 2005).

49 For further discussion, see chapter 10.

50 Tsong-kha-pa presents the four ways to gather disciples much later in the *Great Treatise* (2: 225). His Holiness chooses to bring this list forward and explain a portion of it here in relation to the section on the qualities of a reliable spiritual teacher (1: 70).

51 The ten nonvirtuous actions are killing, stealing, sexual misconduct, lying, divisive speech, offensive speech, senseless speech, covetousness, malice, and wrong views. See Tsong-kha-pa's *Great Treatise* 1: 216-227.

52 Translated by Christian Lindtner in *Nagarjuniana* (Delhi: Motilal Banarsidass, 1987) and also available in English at www.bodhicitta.net.

53 Verse 73.

54 See His Holiness's answers to questions about this point below, pages 35–37.

55 Referring to Tulku Sungrab (b. 1903?), who was recognized as the incarnation of Alak Dongak Gyatso and enthroned at Nyen-mo Monastery. His writing attempts to synthesize the views and terminology of the Nyingma tantric texts with the tantras associated with the other (later) Tibetan sects.

56 Verse 192; Rinchen and Sonam's translation, *Aryadeva's Four Hundred Stanzas*, 195.

57 The Tibetan of this passage of the *Commentary on the Compendium of Valid Cognition* is P5709, 81.4.3.

58 As becomes clear through references to the "purpose of emptiness" below (pages 141–142), His Holiness is referring to the *Fundamental Wisdom of the Middle Way* (24.7), where Nagarjuna introduces his refutation of essentialists who think that emptiness precludes cause-and-effect relationships, stating that those who hold this view do not understand emptiness, nor the purpose and significance of the Buddha's teaching of emptiness.

59 This refers to the second verse of the *Sputartha* (*'grel ba don gsal*), the best known of Haribhadra's commentaries explaining the Perfection of Wisdom sutras as organized by the *Ornament of Clear Realization* (*Abhisamayalamkara*), a text Maitreya is believed to have revealed to Asanga. An English translation of this verse appears in all caps embedded within Gareth Sparham's translation of Tsong-kha-pa's *Golden Garland of Eloquence,* vol. 1 (Fremont, Calif.: Jain Publishing Company, 2008), 27-28. It is believed that Maitreya initially appeared to Asanga as a maggot-covered dog. Asanga cut flesh from his body to make a safe place for the maggots; he prepared to remove them carefully from the dog with his tongue. Maitreya then changed his form and became Asanga's teacher. Perhaps with this in mind, Haribhadra says that the *Ornament of Clear Realization* arises from Asanga's attachment to living beings. Tsong-kha-pa glosses "attachment" here as "surpassing love, like the compassion felt by great bodhisattvas."

60 His Holiness is here referring to Tsong-kha-pa's explanation in his *Golden Garland of Eloquence.* The relevant portion will appear in volume four of Sparham's translation, forthcoming from Jain Publishing Company. (For the Tibetan, see P6150,

vol.154; this passage is in chapter 5 at 181a in Lhasa edition from *gzhol par khang*). The sutra to which Tsong-kha-pa is referring is the *Rice Seedling Sutra;* see N. Ross Reat's *The Salistamba Sutra* (Delhi: Motilal Banarsidass, 1993).

The twelve links of dependent arising are: (1) ignorance, (2) volitional action, (3) consciousness, (4) name and form, (5) the six sources, (6) contact, (7) feeling, (8) craving, (9) grasping, (10) potential existence, (11) birth, (12) aging and death. Ignorance refers to grasping at a reified personal self, this being antithetical to knowing how karma works and the nature of reality. Volitional action means contaminated karma, actions that are based on mental afflictions. Consciousness here refers to a primary or main mental consciousness that is infused with karmic propensities. Name and form refer to the mental and physical aggregates. The six sources refer to the capacity to experience five sense objects and objects of mental consciousness. Contact refers to the coming together of object, sensory capacity, and consciousness. Feeling means pleasant, painful, or neutral experience. Craving refers to mental factors of not wanting to be separated from what is pleasant and attractive and to be separated from what is painful and unattractive. Grasping is a strong increase of craving, including yearning after and attachment to attractive sense objects, bad views, etc. Potential existence is the activated propensity to take rebirth. Birth refers to the first moment of consciousness in a new rebirth. Aging and death are the maturation, transformation, and casting aside of aggregates. (Tsong-kha-pa's *Great Treatise*: 1: 315-319.) See also mention of twelve links below on pages 55 and 59 and chapter 8.

For explanations of the twelve links, see His Holiness's *The Meaning of Life* (Boston: Wisdom Publications, 2000) and Geshe Sonam Rinchen and Ruth Sonam's *How Karma Works* (Ithaca, N.Y.: Snow Lion Publications, 2006).

61 Here His Holiness is referring to the teaching that cyclic existence operates via the twelve links of dependent arising. See previous note.

62 The four embodiments are a buddha's embodiment of truth as wisdom (a buddha's perfect wisdom), embodiment of truth as nature (ultimate reality), embodiment as blissful form (a buddha's divine body in a pure land), and embodiment as emanated form (a buddha's compassionate appearance to beings within cyclic existence).

63 Verses 4-8 as numbered in Lindtner's *Nagarjuniana*, 103-105; verses 5-9 as numbered at www.tibetanclassics.org/pdfs/SixtyStanzas.pdf.

64 Arhats are persons who have reached liberation from cyclic existence through a non-Mahayana Buddhist path, a path on which they have been motivated primarily by seeking peace for themselves rather than the happiness of all beings.

65 These thirty-seven are qualities conducive to or correlated with enlightenment. In the *Anguttara Nikaya* (7.67), the Buddha says, "Monks, although a monk who does not apply himself to the meditative development of his mind may wish, 'Oh, that my mind might be free from the taints by nonclinging!' yet his mind will not be freed. Why? Because he has not developed his mind. Not developed it in what? In the four foundations of mindfulness, the four right kinds of striving, the four bases of success, the five spiritual faculties, the five spiritual powers, the seven factors of enlightenment, and the Noble Eightfold Path."

66 The six perfections are generosity, ethical discipline, patience, joyous perseverance, meditative stabilization, and wisdom. Tsong-kha-pa (2: 85-224), like many other

Mahayana writers, uses this set to summarize the practices of the bodhisattva path. These practices constitute "perfections" insofar as they are both motivated by the wish to attain perfect enlightenment for the sake of helping all beings and imbued with an understanding of emptiness.

67 Tsong-kha-pa is among those who divide Buddhist tantric texts and practice traditions into four classes, of which the highest yoga tantras are the highest. See the Dalai Lama et al., *Tantra in Tibet* (Ithaca, N.Y.: Snow Lion Publications, 1987).

68 For this and the next sentence, see Rosemarie Fuchs's translation of the *Sublime Continuum* in *Buddha Nature: The Mahayana Uttaratantra Shastra with Commentary* (Ithaca, N.Y.: Snow Lion Publications, 2000), 21.

69 The four seals of Buddhist doctrine are: all conditioned phenomena are impermanent; all contaminated phenomena are in the nature of suffering; all phenomena are empty and devoid of self; nirvana is true peace. His Holiness discusses these below (pages 60-61, 79-80, and 139). His point here is that when the person who truly understands the Dharma goes for refuge, the objects of refuge—the three jewels—are understood in the light of the four seals. This makes it distinctively Buddhist.

70 *Fundamental Wisdom of the Middle Way*, 18.5. See Jay L. Garfield's translation, *The Fundamental Wisdom of the Middle Way* (New York: Oxford University Press, 1995), 248. See also His Holiness's comments on this passage in his *The Middle Way*, 77-80.

71 The Tibetan for this passage is P5709, 86.1.3.

72 See Gareth Sparham's translation, *Abhisamayalamkara with Vrtti and Aloka*, vol. 3 (Fremont, Calif.: Jain Publishing Company, 2009), 7 and 117.

73 Losang Chogyen refers to Losang Chokyi Gyaltsen (1570-1662), who was a teacher of the Fifth Dalai Lama, Ngawang Losang. The Fifth Dalai Lama recognized this scholar as a Panchen Lama; Panchen means "great scholar." Losang Chokyi Gyaltsen's three prior incarnations were then posthumously recognized as Panchen Lamas. Thus, some sources call him the first Panchen Lama and others (by including the retroactive designees) count him as the fourth. The seventh (or tenth) Panchen Lama (1938-1989) had a similar name: Losang Trinley Lhundrup Chokyi Gyaltsen.

For the Dalai Lama's explanation of Losang Chokyi Gyaltsen's stages of the path teachings, see *Path to Bliss* (Ithaca, N.Y.: Snow Lion Publications, 1991).

74 Within cyclic existence, there are three realms: the desire realm, the form realm, and the formless realm. We reside in the desire realm. The form and formless realms are inhabited exclusively by beings living their entire lives absorbed unwaveringly in meditation on a single object. The four levels of the form realm and the four levels of the formless realm correspond to the different levels of meditation.

75 Verse 64 in David Ross Komito's *Nagarjuna's Seventy Stanzas* (Ithaca, N.Y.: Snow Lion Publications, 1999), 94 and 175; and verse 64 in Lindtner's *Nagarjuniana*, 63.

76 Verses 135-136 in Rinchen and Sonam's *Aryadeva's Four Hundred Stanzas*, 159-160. The *Great Treatise* (3: 207) cites the first of these two verses from Aryadeva's *Four Hundred*.

77 Verse 3 in Komito's *Nagarjuna's Seventy Stanzas*, 79 and 101-102; verse 3 in Lindtner's *Nagarjuniana*, 35.

78 See note 60 above.

79 Verse 23 of *Praise to the Buddha for Teaching Dependent Origination*. See Thupten Jinpa's translation at www.tibetanclassics.org/Jinpa_Translations.html and Gavin Kilty's translation in *The Splendor of an Autumn Moon*, 227. His Holiness's oral teachings on this text are available on the DVD *In Praise of Dependent Origination* (San Jose, Calif.: Gyuto Vajrayana Center, 2009).

80 Verse 190. Rinchen and Sonam's *Aryadeva's Four Hundred Stanzas*, 193.

81 Sugata, meaning "Well-gone One," is an honorific title for the Buddha.

82 See "Concise Meaning of the Stages of the Path" in Geshe Wangyal's *Door of Liberation* (Boston: Wisdom Publications, 1995), 176-177.

83 P5709, 87.5.5.

84 In the term *ma rig pa*, usually translated as "ignorance," *rig pa* means "knowledge" or "wisdom" and *ma* is a negative particle. The same is true of the Sanskrit equivalent *avidya*, wherein *vidya* means "knowledge" and *a-* is a negative prefix.

85 The *King of Concentrations Sutra* (*Samadhirajasutra*) is one scriptural source for the famous list of four seals. Geshe Yeshe Tapkay traces it also to *The Question of the Naga King Sagara Sutra* (*glu'i rgyal po rgya mthso zhu pa'i mdo*). An English translation of this brief text, from a Chinese version, appears at http://www.fodian.net/world/0599.html; Taisho 0599.

86 See *Abhidharmasamuccaya*, translated into English by Sara Boin-Webb from an earlier French translation by Walpola Rahula (Fremont, Calif.: Asian Humanities Press, 2001).

87 As translated by Art Engle in *The Inner Science of Buddhist Practice* (Ithaca, N.Y.: Snow Lion Publications, 2009). It is also found in Stefan Anacker's *Seven Works by Vasubandhu* (Delhi: Motilal Banarsidass, 1984).

88 See discussion of the three capacities of beings in chapter 7.

89 According to this story, the bodhisattva who would later become Shakyamuni Buddha was in a past lifetime the student of a teacher who gave instructions on why it was virtuous to steal. While the other students agreed to steal, the future buddha remained silent. Asked to explain his silence, he stated that stealing did not seem right because it went against the general teachings. The teacher—who had been testing his students—then praised him as the best student. See *Great Treatise* 1: 385-386.

90 The six aspects of preparation (1: 94-99) are: (1) clean your place and properly arrange representations of the Buddha's body, speech, and mind; (2) obtain offerings without deceit and arrange them beautifully; (3) assume a full or half-lotus posture, taking refuge and developing the spirit of enlightenment; (4) imagine as seated in space before you the guru lineages, the buddhas, and the bodhisattvas; (5) carry out the seven branches of worship so as to accumulate merit and wisdom while purifying your mind of obscurations; and (6) make requests or supplication, requests for blessings. The seven branches of worship (1: 94-99) are: (1) obeisance to the enlightened ones, (2) making offerings to them, (3) confession of one's sins, (4) rejoicing in the merit of enlightened beings, (5) imploring them to teach the Dharma, (6) supplicating them to continue teaching for eons, and (7) dedicating the merit of your actions to complete enlightenment of all.

91 Tsong-kha-pa's *Great Treatise* (3: 329) briefly describes these four but they are not prominent in the structure of the text. They are crucial in the Nyingma

philosophies of Rong-zom and Mi-pham, as well as in the teaching of Jamgon Kongtrul. See Heidi I. Köppl's *Establishing Appearances as Divine* (Ithaca, N.Y.: Snow Lion Publications, 2008), chapter 4 and Matthew T. Kapstein's *Reason's Traces* (Boston: Wisdom Publications, 2001), chapter 13.

92 The conventional spirit of enlightenment refers to the aspiration to attain buddhahood for the sake of all living beings. The ultimate spirit of enlightenment is the bodhisattva's realization of emptiness, the ultimate reality. On the six perfections, see note 66 and chapter 10. On the thirty-seven aspects, see note 65.

93 See note 51.

94 See Rinchen and Sonam's *Aryadeva's Four Hundred*, verse 190 on p. 193.

95 Among the ten nonvirtuous actions, three are mental: covetousness, malice, and wrong views. Each corresponds to one of the primary afflictions known as mental poisons: attachment, hostility, and delusion. Covetousness reaches its culmination through the influence of attachment, malice through hostility, and wrong views through delusion. (See *Great Treatise* 1: 227)

96 Excellent versions of this short text are available both in Geshe Sonam Rinchen and Ruth Sonam's *Three Principal Aspects of the Path* (Ithaca, N.Y.: Snow Lion Publications, 1999) and in Sopa and Hopkins's *Cutting Through Appearances.* For the discussion of this point in the latter, see 71-79.

97 Following Atisha's scheme, Tsong-kha-pa (e.g., 1: 135-136) emphasizes that the practices of persons of small and medium capacity are integral to the proper practice of the practices distinctive to a person of great capacity. So the practices appropriate for a person of small capacity are not just for that person, but also for others above that level.

98 P5709, 86.5.2.

99 This section of *Clear Words* (*Prasannapada*) appears in Mervyn Sprung's partial translation as *Lucid Exposition of the Middle Way* (London: Routledge and K. Paul, 1979), 233-246. Compare Tsong-kha-pa's commentary on the same chapter in *Ocean of Reasoning*, translated by Geshe Ngawang Samten and Jay L. Garfield (New York: Oxford University Press, 2006), 469-515.

100 See discussion relating emptiness to the four noble truths in chapter 5.

101 *Byang* means "purified" and *chub* means "comprehension" or "perfect realization."

102 Tsong-kha-pa (1: 298-299) lists the ten as attachment, hostility, pride, ignorance, doubt, the reifying view of the perishing aggregates, extreme view, belief in the supremacy of wrong views, a belief in the supremacy of faulty ethical discipline, and wrong view. His Holiness here classifies just the latter five as view-related afflictions, leaving ignorance and doubt as nonview afflictions. Ignorance within this list then does not have its usual and distinctively Buddhist sense of being a delusion that actively holds a wrong view, but rather has a sense of not knowing certain crucial facts (e.g., the four noble truths.) Tsong-kha-pa (1: 300) makes it clear that he does not think of ignorance as it appears within this list of ten as being the fundamental delusion at the root of cyclic existence. Contrast this with the more typical meaning of ignorance as it appears as the first of the twelve links of dependent origination, below.

103 *Abhidharmasamuccaya*, Boin-Webb (tr.). His Holiness also cites this passage above on page 62.

104 Tsong-kha-pa (3: 206) cites this passage. The Tibetan appears at the very end of *Clear Words* at P5260, 91.5.3-6 and Derge Bstan 'gyur, dbu ma, vol. 'a, 198b5-199a1. The Sanskrit for this passage does not appear in La Vallée Poussin's Sanskrit edition, and Wayman's *Calming the Mind and Discerning the Real* (New York: Columbia University Press, 1978), 465 n. 201, notes that J. W. de Jong (*Oriens Extremus* 9 (1962), 47) attributes the Sanskrit to a different work by Chandrakirti.

105 *Fundamental Wisdom of the Middle Way* 15.2cd; *Garfield's Fundamental Wisdom*, 221.

106 For a general overview of the twelve links, see note 60 above. The particular point His Holiness is making here follows Tsong-kha-pa's (1: 322-323) explanation that these two or three lifetimes need not be, and often may not be, successive. The first lifetime in such a sequence may even be eons before the second one. Existence in an intermediate state (*bardo*) between lives is not counted as a lifetime in these sequences.

107 This is relevant here because immediately above, in discussing the ten afflictions, the nonview afflictions include ignorance that is a simple "not properly knowing" rather than this more usual sense of an active, afflicted, and wrong cognition.

108 This refers to Tsong-kha-pa's interpretation of Chandrakirti's explanation of how karma works in the absence of any inherently existent entity to carry the action's potential from one lifetime to the next. The disintegratedness (*zhig pa*) of the action carries on in an impermanent and functional continuum. The fullest explanation of this is in Daniel Cozort's *Unique Tenets of the Middle Way Consequence School* (Ithaca, N.Y.: Snow Lion Publications, 1998), 181-230.

109 The Kadampa master Pu-chung-wa Shonu Gyaltsen (1041-1106) was a student of Atisha's disciple Drom-don-pa.

110 This follows Tsong-kha-pa's reading of Chandrakirti's form of Madhyamaka. A brief explanation can be found in Cozort's *Unique Tenets*, 258-259. Unlike some systems, wherein the term selflessness of persons refers to an emptiness that is coarser than the selflessness of phenomena, here the term selflessness of persons refers to the same profound emptiness.

111 Dharmakirti's *Commentary on the Compendium of Valid Cognition*, P5709, 87.1.8. His Holiness also cites this passage below on page 139.

112 Chapter 7, verse 30. My rendition here finds inspiration from that appearing within Alex Berzin's website, www.berzinarchives.com.

113 Pabongka (1878-1941) was an extremely charismatic lama and one of the leading figures during the generation of the Thirteenth Dalai Lama. His Holiness's tutors, Ling Rinpoche and Trijang Rinpoche, had both received stages of the path teachings from Pabongka. See the new revised edition of Pabongka Rinpoche's *Liberation in the Palm of Your Hand* (Boston: Wisdom Publications, 2006).

114 Since delivering these teachings, His Holiness has published *Beyond Religion: Ethics for a Whole World* (New York: Houghton Mifflin Harcourt, 2011) in which he details his vision of secular ethics. He there explains (ix-19) that in this context "secular" does not at all mean excluding religion, but rather finding a common ethical ground among those of many different religions and those with no religion.

115 Referring to the eighth chapter of *Engaging in the Bodhisattva Deeds*, especially verses 8.104-105. There Shantideva poses himself the question: "But with

compassion there is much suffering. Why strive to develop it?" He responds, "As compared to the suffering of all these beings, how could the suffering of compassion be so great? If the suffering of many disappears through the suffering of one, then a compassionate person would be willing to bear it for the sake of herself and others."

116 See the translation by Thurman et al. as *The Universal Vehicle Discourse Literature*, 32.

117 See chapter 5 and the first half of chapter 7.

118 *Engaging in the Bodhisattva Deeds*, 8.118.

119 See discussion on pages 14–16 and note 62.

120 See the Dalai Lama's *Essence of the Heart Sutra*, 128-129.

121 Disciples, or "hearers" (*nyan thos*), refers to those who seek peace mainly for themselves by listening to and following the teachings of the Buddha. Self-enlightened ones (*rang sangs rgyas*), or solitary realizers (*rang rgyal*), refers to those who seek peace mainly for themselves through solitary practice. Both follow paths that are not the bodhisattva path and attain enlightenment as arhats in a profound peace (nirvana) that is not the perfect enlightenment of a buddha. See Daniel Cozort and Craig Preston's *Buddhist Philosophy* (Ithaca, N.Y.: Snow Lion Publications, 2003), 275-278.

122 See note 90 and, for somewhat more detail, *Great Treatise* 1: 94-98.

123 This is 8.129-130. The next verse below is 8.131. Tsong-kha-pa cites these verses at *Great Treatise* 2: 52.

124 This refers to *Engaging in the Bodhisattva Deeds* 1.7 and the surrounding verses.

124 A traditional prayer derived from *Engaging in the Bodhisattva Deeds*, including 2.26 and 3.22.

126 This is *Engaging in the Bodhisattva Deeds* 3.26; what follows directly below is 3.27.

127 See page 14.

128 Verse 60 in *Sixty Stanzas of Reasoning* as the verses are translated and numbered at: http://www.tibetanclassics.org/pdfs/SixtyStanzas.pdf.

129 The *Great Treatise* explores in greater depth the theme of this short section at 2: 85-99.

130 These ten are listed in note 51.

131 For the quote from *Praise to the Buddha for Teaching Dependent Origination*, compare Kilty's *Splendor of an Autumn Moon*, 235, and Berzin's translation at http://samforbes.wordpress.com/in-praise-of-dependent-arising-from-berzin-archives. In the final sentence, His Holiness refers to a subsequent passage in which Tsong-kha-pa says he found peace when he saw the orb of Chandrakirti's wisdom moving through the sky of the Buddha's words and dispelling the darkness of extreme views.

132 On the preeminence of the Buddha among the three jewels, see Fuchs's translation of the *Sublime Continuum* as *Buddha Nature: The Mahayana Uttaratantra Shastra with Commentary*, 20-22. Since the state of buddhahood is the ultimate in wisdom, only the buddhas have attained the state of the level of no-more-learning. Thus, the distinction between learner and nonlearner jewels applies only to the Dharma and the Sangha. The learner Dharma jewel is true paths and true cessations as practiced on the path; the learner Sangha jewel is a person who has actualized these—that is, has attained a nirvana—but has not yet become a fully enlightened buddha. The

nonlearner Dharma jewel is the final completion of true paths and true cessations in the mind of a Buddha; and the nonlearner Sangha is the person, the Buddha, who has brought true paths and true cessations to completion.

133 See note 66.

134 See the Dalai Lama's own presentation of Kamalashila's second *Stages of Meditation* in his *Stages of Meditation* (Ithaca, N.Y.: Snow Lion Publications, 2003).

135 Vairochana is an important buddha in many tantric and nontantric Mahayana traditions and texts.

136 Dzogchen is a system for directly introducing students to the fundamental (nature of) mind. It is closely associated with the Nyingma lineage of Tibetan Buddhism. For the Dalai Lama's Dzogchen teachings, see his *Dzogchen: The Heart Essence of the Great Perfection* (Ithaca, N.Y.: Snow Lion Publications, 2004). Regarding the Kalachakra tantric practice, see the Dalai Lama's *Kalachakra Tantra: Rite of Initiation* (Boston: Wisdom Publications, 1999).

137 The practices of highest yoga tantra involve controlling vital energies, or winds (*rlung*). The body is animated by the flow of these subtle energies through thousands of subtle (invisible) but physical channels. Along with these winds and channels, the subtle body of a human also includes white and red drops, subtle essences. See Dan Cozort's *Highest Yoga Tantra* (Ithaca, N.Y.: Snow Lion Publications, 1986), 42-45 and 72-73.

138 Mahamudra is a system for directly introducing students to the fundamental (nature of) mind; it is most closely associated with the Kagyu lineage of Tibetan Buddhism. For the Dalai Lama's Mahamudra teachings, see his *The Gelug-Kagyü Tradition of Mahamudra* (Ithaca, N.Y.: Snow Lion Publications, 1997).

139 The mind of clear light is the subtlest form of consciousness in Buddhist tantra. It becomes manifest when the subtle energies of the body dissolve in the central channel. See Cozort's *Highest Yoga Tantra*, 75-76.

140 Tsong-kha-pa follows the Prasangika Madhyamaka system of Chandrakirti, which rejects any claim that a single instant of mind can know itself.

141 Ultimately, the mind—like all other phenomena—is empty. Even conventionally, it has no intrinsic nature such as would allow it to exist in and of itself. Like all other existents, it exists only by way of its interdependence with other things. However, just as fire is hot and ice is cold, the mind also has a distinctive character conventionally.

142 Tsong-kha-pa (*Great Treatise* 3: 73-75) describes these nine mental states as: (1) mental placement, (2) continuous placement, (3) patched placement, (4) close placement, (5) taming, (6) pacification, (7) complete pacification, (8) single-pointed attention, and (9) balanced placement. On these and the eight faults, etc., see Leah Zahler's *Study and Practice of Meditation* (Ithaca, N.Y.: Snow Lion Publications, 2009), chapter 4.

143 Cyclic existence includes three realms, the desire realm (where we reside) and two higher realms: the form realm and the formless realm. The form and formless realms are attained through meditative prowess and are characterized by long lifetimes free from physical misery. On the other hand, the beings residing there are not necessarily any more enlightened or spiritually advanced. On the comparative suffering of humans, demigods, and gods in the desire realm with the gods of the higher realms,

see Tsong-kha-pa's *Great Treatise* 1: 292-295. For a quick introduction to Buddhist cosmology, see Damien Keown's *Buddhism: A Very Short Introduction* (Oxford: Oxford University Press, 2000), chapter 3.

144 P5709, 87.2.5.

145 This refers to Chandrakirti's *Commentary on the Middle Way* (*Madhyamakavatara*), 6.164; see the Padmakara Translation Group's translation as *Introduction to the Middle Way* (Boston: Shambhala, 2002), 91.

146 Tsong-kha-pa cites this crucial verse three times in the *Great Treatise*: near the beginning of the serenity section (3: 23), at the start of the insight section (3: 108), and near the end of the insight section (3: 345). Along with the preceding verse, this sutra citation appears in Kamalashila's second *Stages of Meditation*; see His Holiness's *Stages of Meditation*, 83-84; note that in that work the source of this sutra citation is incorrectly attributed.

147 P5709, 87.1.8.

148 *Fundamental Wisdom* (18.8) says, "Everything is real and is not real, both real and unreal, neither real nor unreal. This is the Lord Buddha's teaching." Jay L. Garfield's translation, *The Fundamental Wisdom of the Middle Way*, 49.

149 Verse 44: "The Buddhas have purposefully spoken of 'is,' 'is not,' and 'both is and is not.' It is not easy to understand!" Compare Lindtner's *Nagarjuniana*, 55 and Komito's *Nagarjuna's Seventy Stanzas*, 90 and 155-157.

150 See John Powers's translation of this as *Wisdom of Buddha* (Berkeley: Dharma Publishing, 1995).

151 Tsong-kha-pa (3: 113) cites both the *Teachings of Akshayamati* and the *King of Concentrations* sutras as indicating that scriptures teaching emptiness are definitive and those teaching about other phenomena are provisional.

152 Nagarjuna's sixfold Analytic Collections (*rigs tshogs drug*) are: *Fundamental Wisdom of the Middle Way*, *Sixty Stanzas of Reasoning*, *Seventy Stanzas on Emptiness*, *Refutation of Objections*, *Finely Woven*, and *Precious Garland*.

153 This famous verse is cited in the *Stainless Light* (*Vimalaprabha*), a commentary on the *Kalachakra Tantra*, as well as in Shantarakshita's *Reality Compendium* (*Tattvasamgraha*). Shantarakshita does not say what sutra it comes from. It is sometimes cited by modern Theravada teachers and is frequently said to occur in the Pali canon, but I have not seen the citation. A passage that appears to be the same original, translated into Tibetan slightly differently, appears in a tantra called *The Very Powerful Lord of Tantras* (*dpal stobs po che'i rgyud gyi rgyal po*) in Tarthang Tulku's *Derge Kanjur*, rgyud, ga, 216b.6; vol.28, 447-3-6.

154 *Sixty Stanzas* (51-52ab) reads: "Having found a locus, one is caught by the twisting snake of the afflictions; those whose minds have no locus will not be caught. How could the deadly poison of the afflictions fail to rise in those whose minds possess a locus?" See: www.tibetanclassics.org/pdfs/SixtyStanzas.pdf.

155 See the Dalai Lama's *The Universe in a Single Atom* for more on his view of Buddhism and quantum physics. For a Tibetan Buddhism-derived critique of materialist reductionism in Western science, see B. Alan Wallace and Brian Hodel's *Embracing Mind* (Boston: Shambhala, 2008).

156 This "emptiness of other" (*gzhan stong*) approach, a widely influential tradition, was popularized by the Jo-nang teacher Shay-rap Gyal-tsen (1292-1361).

157 *Dharmadhatu-stotra.*

158 That is, they present the ultimate in positive or even absolutist terms, rather than as a mere absence of inherent existence. For example, Fuchs's translation of the *Sublime Continuum* as *Buddha Nature: The Mahayana Uttaratantra Shastra with Commentary*, 52: "The state of the Muni [=Buddha] being of uncreated nature has been fully pacified since beginningless time . . . it is inexpressible since it consists of the absolute [truth] . . . it is absolute since it cannot be scrutinized. It is inscrutable because it cannot be inferentially deduced."

159 On Losang Chogyen, see note 73. For the Dalai Lama's Mahamudra teachings, including a translation of the text to which he here refers, see his *The Gelug-Kagyü Tradition of Mahamudra.* For scholars, see Roger Jackson's "The dGe ldan–bKa' brgyud Tradition of Mahamudra" in Guy Newland, ed., *Changing Minds* (Ithaca, N.Y.: Snow Lion Publications, 2001).

160 This refers to the distinction between ways of presenting the teachings that are *specific to an individual* as distinct from approaches that *take into account the overall structure of the path.* See discussion on pages 29–31.

161 The translation of the relevant passages of *Clear Words* appears at *Great Treatise* 3: 120-121. Compare Sprung's *Lucid Exposition of the Middle Way*, 165.

162 Rinchen and Sonam's *Aryadeva's Four Hundred Stanzas*, verse 350 on p. 275.

163 Referring to "Meditations to Sever the Ego" from *Songs on Mind Training* by the Seventh Dalai Lama, Kelsang Gyatso (1708-1757); see especially verses 2-5. Translated by Glenn Mullin in *Meditations to Transform the Mind* (Ithaca, N.Y.: Snow Lion Publications, 1999), 110.

164 On Gung-tang, see note 16. This and all subsequent references to him refer to his *Meaningful Praises of Tsong-kha-pa* (*tsong kha pa'i bstod pa don dang ldan pa*) (Taipei: The Corporate Body of the Buddha Educational Foundation, 2002).

165 As presented in chapter 22 of the *Fundamental Wisdom of the Middle Way.* See Garfield's *The Fundamental Wisdom of the Middle Way*, 276-277.

166 Chandrakirti presents the sevenfold reasoning in chapter 6 of his *Commentary on the Middle Way.* Tsong-kha-pa's presentation of these arguments is found in the *Great Treatise* at 3: 289-300.

167 Tsong-kha-pa's *Great Treatise* (3: 144) also makes precisely this point: "Most Tibetans who claim to be Madhyamikas seem to agree with the essentialists' assertion that if an argument refutes intrinsic nature, it must also refute cause and effect. Yet unlike essentialists, these Tibetans seem to be pleased that reason refutes cause and effect, taking this to be the Madhyamaka system." Gung-tang's comment is from *Meaningful Praises of Tsong-kha-pa,* 1-2.

168 These two sentences refer to the *Fundamental Wisdom of the Middle Way*, 24.18; Garfield's *The Fundamental Wisdom of the Middle Way*, 69. The Tibetan for "fundamental middle way" here is *gzhi 'dbu ma.*

169 *Fundamental Wisdom of the Middle Way*, 24.7; Garfield's *The Fundamental Wisdom of the Middle Way*, 68.

170 *Fundamental Wisdom of the Middle Way*, 24.18; Garfield's *The Fundamental Wisdom of the Middle Way*, 69.

171 Referring to a passage from the *Questions of the Naga King Anavatapta Sutra* that Tsong-kha-pa cites and comments upon at *Great Treatise* 3: 188.

172 *Fundamental Wisdom of the Middle Way*, 24.18; Garfield's *The Fundamental Wisdom of the Middle Way*, 69.

173 The "diamond slivers" refers to the argument that something—e.g., a sprout, a person's body, etc.—is not intrinsically produced because it is not produced from itself, from something intrinsically other, from both, or without cause. This argument is found in the first verse of Nagarjuna's *Fundamental Wisdom*; see Garfield's *The Fundamental Wisdom of the Middle Way*, 3. For an example of a Tibetan-tradition-based explanation, see Jeffrey Hopkins's *Meditation on Emptiness* (Boston: Wisdom Publications, 1996), 57-59.

174 See Sopa and Hopkins's *Cutting Through Appearances*, 101-102.

175 Nagarjuna's *Precious Garland*, verse 80; see Hopkins's *Nagarjuna's Precious Garland*, 104.

176 His Holiness here makes reference to and interprets verses 81 and 82 of Nagarjuna's *Precious Garland*.

177 Chandrakirti's *Commentary on the Middle Way*, 6.158-160. See the Padmakara Translation Group's translation as *Introduction to the Middle Way*, 90.

178 Chandrakirti's *Commentary on the Middle Way*, 6.185. See the Padmakara Translation Group's translation as *Introduction to the Middle Way*, 94.

179 Nagarjuna's *Fundamental Wisdom* 24.10ab; see Garfield's *The Fundamental Wisdom of the Middle Way*, 68.

180 Chandrakirti's *Commentary on the Middle Way*, 6.80; see the Padmakara Translation Group's translation as *Introduction to the Middle Way*, 79.

181 Above (pages 150–151), His Holiness says that, following Gung-tang, "when we cultivate the view of emptiness, we set out to understand the nature of things. In that process, we do not find any inherent existence. This nonfinding of inherent existence in itself constitutes the negation of inherent existence."

182 Referring to the *King of Concentrations Sutra*. Tsong-kha-pa's explanation of this passage is at *Great Treatise* 3: 164.

183 These four types of reliable knowledge are enumerated by a school of Hindu philosophy called Nyaya. Nagarjuna's *Refutation of Objections* (verses 40-46) criticizes the realist philosophy underlying this Nyaya presentation of reliable knowledge. Tsong-kha-pa and His Holiness follow Chandrakirti's interpretation of Nagarjuna, according to which Nagarjuna's critique of Nyaya is not taken to preclude the operation of these four types of reliable knowledge at the conventional level. Chandrakirti's *Clear Words* explicitly says that objects in the world are known, conventionally, by these four.

184 Verse 52 introduces this mirage analogy, with implications drawn out over verses 53-56. See Hopkins's *Nagarjuna's Precious Garland*, 101.

185 For more on this, see Hopkins's *Tsong-kha-pa's Final Exposition of Wisdom*, 41, note c; and Jeffrey Hopkins's *Maps of the Profound* (Ithaca, N.Y.: Snow Lion Publications, 2004), 890.

186 A syllogism here refers to a formal argument in the form "Regarding X, Y is the case because of Z; as in the case of A." An autonomous syllogism is a syllogism in which both the parties in a debate verify the elements of the syllogism with the same type of reliable knowledge, whereby the syllogism can work on its own to bring about transformed understanding in the person to whom it is addressed.

Bhavaviveka insists that explanations of Nagarjuna's arguments should be formulated in this manner, faulting Buddhapalita for failing to do so. Chandrakirti and his followers critique Bhavaviveka's approach, arguing that when Madhyamikas debate with others about emptiness, syllogistic reasoning cannot function autonomously because Madhyamikas have fundamentally different ideas about the type of reliable knowledge verifying the elements of the syllogism.

This is inevitably a difficult topic; for a relatively accessible account, see Guy Newland's *Introduction to Emptiness* (Ithaca, N.Y.: Snow Lion Publications, 2008), 77-85.

187 Samkhya is one of the six traditional schools of Hindu philosophy. It is strongly dualist, accepting two fundamental realities: Person (*purusha*) and Nature (*prakriti*). Person is eternal and uncaused. Samkhya argues that since all phenomenal events are permutations of Nature, effects already exist latent within their causes. Thus, the Buddhists attribute to Samkhya and then critique the position that *things are produced from themselves* in the sense that things are manifestations or transformations of earlier nonmanifest forms of themselves.

188 On the difference between Tsong-kha-pa's two explanations of where Bhavaviveka goes wrong, and a scholarly explanation of *why* Tsong-kha-pa's reading changed, see Hopkins's "A Tibetan Delineation of Different Views of Emptiness in the Middle Way School" in *Tibet Journal* 14, no.1 (1989), 10-43.

189 Chapter 6, verses 34-36. See the Padmakara Translation Group's translation as *Introduction to the Middle Way*, 73 and 204-210.

190 Here His Holiness again refers to the doctrine of the "emptiness of other" found in Jonang and other Tibetan Buddhist lineages, but criticized in Tsong-kha-pa's *Great Treatise* 3: 201. On Jonang, see note 44.

191 *Fundamental Wisdom of the Middle Way*, 18.2cd; Garfield's *The Fundamental Wisdom of the Middle Way*, 48.

192 These are: liking (1) rewards, (2) pleasure, (3) praise, and (4) good reputation; disliking (5) lack of reward, (6) pain, (7) criticism, and (8) anything that harms our reputation.

193 *Vaidalya-prakarana*, *passim*. A useful summary of the arguments of this text is found in Richard H. Jones's *Nagarjuna* (New York: Jackson Square Books, 2010), 79-90. See also the translation in Fernando Tola and Carmen Dragonetti's *Nagarjuna's Refutation of Logic* (Delhi: Motilal Banarsidass, 1995).

194 Verse 12, my translation. For an excellent translation and commentary on this text, see Geshe Sonam Rinchen and Ruth Sonam's *The Three Principal Aspects of the Path* (Ithaca, N.Y.: Snow Lion Publications, 2010). This verse is on page 122.

195 See Elizabeth Napper's *Dependent Arising and Emptiness* (Boston: Wisdom Publications, 2003) and "Ethics as the Basis of a Tantric Tradition" in Guy Newland, ed., *Changing Minds*, 107-131, for further analysis of how Tsong-kha-pa uses his sources in the *Great Treatise*.